"十三五"全国高等院校民航服务专业规划

民航面试英语教程

—————— 主　编◎黄　晨

副主编◎邱景翎　李　响

English Course for Civil Aviation Interview

清华大学出版社

北京

内 容 简 介

本书以实用为原则，共分为四单元，内容涉及面试前的准备，以及面试过程中的各个环节。第一单元为如何写好求职简历，赢得面试机会。主要针对面试前准备部分的训练。第二单元为如何进行自我介绍，取得良好开端。主要为面试中初试部分的训练。第三单元为如何巧答面试难题，博得评委青睐。包括家庭情况、教育背景、品德个性、兴趣爱好和职业规划，主要为面试中复试部分的训练。第四单元为如何应对专业问答，展现技能水平。主要为面试中终审部分的训练。每一单元的设置包括知识点剖析、单词练习、重点句式学习、实战范例、技巧讲解和扩展阅读，素材丰富，体裁多样，语言规范。

本书既适合中、高职院校空中乘务、航空服务、旅游英语等相近相关专业学生使用，也可供民航服务及其他服务行业从业人员参考。

图书在版编目（CIP）数据

民航面试英语教程 / 黄晨主编. —北京：清华大学出版社，2019（2025.7 重印）
（"十三五"全国高等院校民航服务专业规划教材）
ISBN 978-7-302-52213-3

Ⅰ.①民⋯　Ⅱ.①黄⋯　Ⅲ.①民用航空–英语–口语–高等学校–教材　Ⅳ.①F56

中国版本图书馆CIP数据核字（2019）第016130号

责任编辑：杜春杰
封面设计：刘　超
版式设计：王凤杰
责任校对：马军令
责任印制：丛怀宇

出版发行：清华大学出版社
　　　　网　　　址：https://www.tup.com.cn, https://www.wqxuetang.com
　　　　地　　　址：北京清华大学学研大厦A座　　　邮　　编：100084
　　　　社 总 机：010-83470000　　　　邮　　购：010-62786544
　　　　投稿与读者服务：010-62776969, c-service@tup.tsinghua.edu.cn
　　　　质 量 反 馈：010-62772015, zhiliang@tup.tsinghua.edu.cn
印 装 者：三河市龙大印装有限公司
经　　销：全国新华书店
开　　本：185mm×260mm　　　印　　张：9.75　　　字　　数：229千字
版　　次：2019年6月第1版　　　印　　次：2025年7月第8次印刷
定　　价：49.80元

产品编号：081557-01

"十三五"全国高等院校民航服务专业规划教材
丛书主编及专家指导委员会

丛 书 总 主 编　刘　永（北京中航未来科技集团有限公司董事长兼总裁）

丛 书 副 总 主 编　马晓伟（北京中航未来科技集团有限公司常务副总裁）

丛 书 副 总 主 编　郑大地（北京中航未来科技集团有限公司教学副总裁）

丛 书 总 主 审　朱益民（原海南航空公司总裁、原中国货运航空公司总裁、原上海航空公司总裁）

丛书英语总主审　王　朔（美国雪城大学、纽约市立大学巴鲁克学院双硕士）

丛 书 总 顾 问　沈泽江（原中国民用航空华东管理局局长）

丛 书 总 执 行 主 编　王益友［江苏民航职业技术学院（筹）院长、教授］

丛 书 艺 术 总 顾 问　万峻池（美术评论家、著名美术品收藏家）

丛书总航空法律顾问　程　颖（荷兰莱顿大学国际法研究生、全国高职高专"十二五"规划教材《航空法规》主审、中国东方航空股份有限公司法律顾问）

丛书专家指导委员会主任

关云飞（长沙航空职业技术学院教授）

张树生（国务院津贴获得者，山东交通学院教授）

刘岩松（沈阳航空航天大学教授）

宋兆宽（河北传媒学院教授）

姚　宝（上海外国语大学教授）

李剑峰（山东大学教授）

孙福万（国家开放大学教授）

张　威（沈阳师范大学教授）

成积春（曲阜师范大学教授）

"十三五"全国高等院校民航服务专业规划教材编委会

出 版 说 明

随着经济的稳步发展，我国已经进入经济新常态的阶段，特别是十九大指出：中国社会主要矛盾已经转化为人民日益增长的美好生活需要和不平衡不充分的发展之间的矛盾，这客观上要求社会服务系统要完善升级。作为公共交通运输的主要组成部分，民航运输在满足人们对美好生活追求和促进国民经济发展中扮演着重要的角色，具有广阔的发展空间。特别是"十三五"期间，国家高度重视民航业的发展，将民航业作为推动我国经济社会发展的重要战略产业，预示着我国民航业将会有更好、更快的发展。从国产化飞机 C919 的试飞，到宽体飞机规划的出台，以及民航发展战略的实施，标志着我国民航业已经步入崭新的发展阶段，这一阶段的特点是以人才为核心，而这一发展模式必将进一步对民航人才质量提出更高的要求。面对民航业发展对人才培养提出的挑战，培养服务于民航业发展的高质量人才，不仅需要转变人才培养观念，创新教育模式，更需要加强人才培养过程中基本环节的建设，而教材建设就是其首要的任务。

我国民航服务专业的学历教育经过十八年的探索与发展，其办学水平、办学结构、办学规模、办学条件和师资队伍等方面都发生了巨大的变化，专业建设水平稳步提高，适应民航发展的人才培养体系初步形成。但我们应该清醒地看到，目前我国民航服务类专业的人才培养仍存在着诸多问题，特别是专业人才培养质量仍不能适应民航发展对人才的需求，人才培养的规模与高质量人才短缺的矛盾仍很突出。而目前相关专业教材的开发还处于探索阶段，缺乏系统性与规范性。已出版的民航服务类专业教材，在吸收民航服务类专业研究成果方面做出了有益的尝试，涌现出不同层次的系列教材，推动了民航服务的专业建设与人才培养，但从总体来看，民航服务类教材的建设仍落后于民航业对专业人才培养的实践要求，教材建设已成为相关人才培养的瓶颈。这就需要以引领和服务专业发展为宗旨，系统总结民航服务实践经验与教学研究成果，开发全面反映民航服务职业特点、符合人才培养规律和满足教学需要的系统性专业教材，以积极、有效地推进民航服务专业人才的培养工作。

基于上述思考，编委会经过两年多的实际调研与反复论证，在广泛征询民航业内专家的意见与建议，总结我国民航服务类专业教育的研究成果后，结合我国民航服务业的发展趋势，致力于编写出一套系统的、具有一定权威性和实用性的民航服务类系列教材，为推进我国民航服务人才的培养尽微薄之力。

本系列教材由沈阳航空航天大学、南昌航空大学、郑州航空工业管理学院、上海民航职业技术学院、长沙航空职业技术学院、西安航空职业技术学院、中原工学院、上海外国语大学、山东大学、大连外国语大学、沈阳师范大学、曲阜师范大学、湖南艺术职业学院、陕西师范大学、兰州大学、云南大学、四川大学、湖南民族职业学院、江西青年职业学院、天津交通职业学院、潍坊职业学院、南京旅游职业学院等多所高校的众多资深专家和学者共同打造，还邀请了多名原中国东方航空公司、原中国南方航空公司、原中国国际航空公司和原海南航空公司中从事多年乘务工作的乘务长和乘务员参与教材的编写。

目前，我国民航服务类的专业教育呈现着多元化、多层次的办学格局，各类学校的办学模式也呈现出个性化的特点，在人才培养体系、课程设置以及课程内容等方面，各学校之间存在着一定的差异，对教材也有不同的需求。为了能够更好地满足不同办学层次、教学模式对教材的需要，本套教材主要突出以下特点。

第一，兼顾本、专科不同培养层次的教学需要。鉴于近些年我国本科层次民航服务专业办学规模的不断扩大，在教材需求方面显得十分迫切，同时，专科层面的办学已经到了规模化的阶段，完善与更新教材体系和内容迫在眉睫，本套教材充分考虑了各类办学层次的需要，本着"求同存异、个性单列、内容升级"的原则，通过教材体系的科学架构和教材内容的层次化，以达到兼顾民航服务类本、专科不同层次教学之需要。

第二，将最新实践经验和专业研究成果融入教材。服务类人才培养是系统性问题，具有很强的内在规定性，民航服务的实践经验和专业建设成果是教材的基础，本套教材以丰富理论、培养技能为主，力求夯实服务基础、培养服务职业素质，将实践层面行之有效的经验与民航服务类人才培养规律的研究成果有效融合，以提高教材对人才培养的有效性。

第三，落实素质教育理念，注重服务人才培养。习近平总书记在党的十九大报告中强调，"要全面贯彻党的教育方针，落实立德树人根本任务，发展素质教育，推进教育公平，培养德智体美全面发展的社会主义建设者和接班人"，人才以德为先，以社会主义价值观铸就人的灵魂，才能使人才担当重任，也是高校人才培养的基本任务。教育实践表明，素质是人才培养的基础，也是人才职业发展的基石，人才的能力与技能以精神与灵魂为附着，但在传统的民航服务教材体系中，包含素质教育板块的教材较为少见。根据党的教育方针，本套教材的编写考虑到素质教育与专业能力培养的关系，以及素质对职业生涯的潜在影响，首次在我国民航服务专业教学中提出专业教育与人文素质并重，素质决定能力的培养理念，以独特的视野精心打造素质教育教材板块，使教材体系更加系统，强化了教材特色。

第四，必要的服务理论与专业能力培养并重。调研分析表明，忽视服务理论与人文素质所培养出的人才很难有宽阔的职业胸怀与职业精神，其未来的职业生涯发展就会乏力。因此，教材不应仅是对单纯技能的阐述与训练指导，更应该是不淡化专业能力培养的同时，强化行业知识、职业情感、服务机理、职业道德等关系到职业发展潜力的要素的培养，以期培养出高层次和高质量的民航服务人才。

第五，架构适合未来发展需要的课程体系与内容。民航服务具有很强的国际化特点，而我国民航服务的思想、模式与方法也正处于不断创新的阶段，紧紧把握未来民航服务的发展趋势，提出面向未来的解决问题的方案，是本套教材的基本出发点和应该承担的责任。我们力图将未来民航服务的发展趋势、服务思想、服务模式创新、服务理论体系以及服务管理等内容进行重新架构，以期能对我国民航服务人才培养，乃至整个民航服务业的发展起到引领作用。

第六，扩大教材的种类，使教材的选择更加宽泛。鉴于我国目前尚缺乏民航服务专业更高层次办学模式的规范，各学校的人才培养方案各具特点，差异明显，为了使教材更适合于办学的需要，本套教材打破了传统教材的格局，通过课程分割、内容优化和课外外延化等方式，增加了教材体系的课程覆盖面，使不同办学层次、关联专业，可以通过教材合理组合获得完整的专业教材选择机会。

  本套教材规划出版品种大约为四十种,分为: ① 人文素养类教材,包括《大学语文》《应用文写作》《艺术素养》《跨文化沟通》《民航职业修养》《中国传统文化》等。② 语言类教材,包括《民航客舱服务英语教程》《民航客舱实用英语口语教程》《民航实用英语听力教程》《民航播音训练》《机上广播英语》《民航服务沟通技巧》等。③ 专业类教材,包括《民航概论》《民航服务概论》《中国民航常飞客源国概况》《民航危险品运输》《客舱安全管理与应急处置》《民航安全检查技术》《民航服务心理学》《航空运输地理》《民航服务法律实务与案例教程》等。④ 职业形象类教材,包括《空乘人员形体与仪态》《空乘人员职业形象设计与化妆》《民航体能训练》等。⑤ 专业特色类教材,包括《民航服务手语训练》《空乘服务专业导论》《空乘人员求职应聘面试指南》《民航面试英语教程》等。

  为了开发职业能力,编者联合有关 VR 开发公司开发了一些与教材配套的手机移动端 VR 互动资源,学生可以利用这些资源体验真实场景。

  本套教材是迄今为止民航服务类专业较为完整的教材系列之一,希望能借此为我国民航服务人才的培养,乃至我国民航服务水平的提高贡献力量。民航发展方兴未艾,民航教育任重道远,为民航服务事业发展培养高质量的人才是各类人才培养部门的共同责任,相信集民航教育的业内学者、专家之共同智慧,凝聚有识之士心血的这套教材的出版,对加速我国民航服务专业建设、完善人才培养模式、优化课程体系、丰富教学内容,以及加强师资队伍建设能起到一定的推动作用。在教材使用的过程中,我们真诚地希望听到业内专家、学者批评的声音,收到广大师生的反馈意见,以利于进一步提高教材的水平。

丛 书 序

《礼记·学记》曰:"古之王者,建国君民,教学为先。"教育是兴国安邦之本,决定着人类的今天,也决定着人类的未来,企业发展也大同小异,重视人才是企业的成功之道,别无二选。航空经济是现代经济发展的新趋势,是当今世界经济发展的新引擎,民航是经济全球化的主流形态和主导模式,是区域经济发展和产业升级的驱动力。作为发展中的中国民航业,有巨大的发展潜力,其民航发展战略的实施必将成为我国未来经济发展的增长点。

"十三五"期间正值实现我国民航强国战略构想的关键时期,"一带一路"倡议方兴未艾,"空中丝路"越来越宽阔。面对高速发展的民航运输,需要推动持续的创新与变革;同时,基于民航运输的安全性和规范性的特点,其对人才有着近乎苛刻的要求,只有人才培养先行,夯实人才基础,才能抓住国家战略转型与产业升级的巨大机遇,实现民航运输发展的战略目标。经过多年民航服务人才发展的积累,我国建立了较为完善的民航服务人才培养体系,培养了大量服务民航发展的各类人才,保证了我国民航运输业的高速持续发展。与此同时,我国民航人才培养正面临新的挑战,既要通过教育创新,提升人才品质,又需要在人才培养过程中精细化,把人才培养目标落实到人才培养的过程中,而教材作为专业人才培养的基础,需要先行,从而发挥引领作用。教材建设发挥的作用并不局限于专业教育本身,其对行业发展的引领,专业人才的培养方向,人才素质、知识、能力结构的塑造以及职业发展潜力的培养具有不可替代的作用。

我国民航运输发展的实践表明,人才培养决定着民航发展的水平,而民航人才的培养需要社会各方面的共同努力。我们惊喜地看到,清华大学出版社秉承"自强不息,厚德载物"的人文精神,发挥强势的品牌优势,投身到民航服务专业系列教材的开发行列,改变了民航服务教材研发的格局,体现了其对社会责任的担当。

本套教材体系组织严谨,精心策划,高屋建瓴,深入浅出,具有突出的特色。第一,从民航服务人才培养的全局出发,关注了民航服务产业的未来发展趋势,架构了以培养目标为导向的教材体系与内容结构,比较全面地反映了服务人才培养趋势,具有良好的统领性;第二,很好地回归了教材的本质———适用性,体现在每本教材均有独特的视角和编写立意,既有高度的提升、理论的升华,也注重教育要素在课程体系中的细化,具有较强的可用性;第三,引入了职业素质教育的理念,补齐了服务人才素质教育缺少教材的短板,可谓是对传统服务人才培养理念的一次冲击;第四,教材编写人员参与面非常广泛。这反映出本套教材充分体现了当今民航服务专业教育的教学成果和编写者的思考,形成了相互交流的良性机制,势必对全国民航服务类专业的发展起到推动作用。

教材建设是专业人才培养的基础,与其服务的行业的发展交互作用,共同实现人才培养——社会检验的良性循环是助推民航服务人才的动力。希望这套教材能够在民航服务类专业人才培养的实践中，发挥更广泛的积极作用。相信通过不断总结与完善，这套教材一定会成为具有自身特色的、适应我国民航业发展要求的，以及深受读者喜欢的规范教材。

　　此为序。

原海南航空公司总裁、原中国货运航空公司总裁、原上海航空公司总裁

朱益民

2017 年 9 月

前　言

随着中国经济的迅猛发展,民航业也大幅加快了发展的步伐。无论是否服务于国际航线,民航类企业对于空乘人员英语的要求都越来越高,这一点在面试环节中尤为明显。目前,市场上同类面试教材虽然较多,但特别针对航空服务类学生面试英语训练的教材并不多见。本教材的编撰者在前期教学和实践方面均有一定的工作基础,因此,本书更加适合航空服务类专业学生的特点和民航企业岗位的需求。

《民航面试英语教程》以民航职业岗位需求为导向,紧密结合航空公司等民航类企业面试实际,结合民航服务类专业毕业生近年的实际反馈意见,内容深入浅出,通俗易懂,便于掌握。旨在给你一张入场券去开启航空公司的大门,助你旗开得胜、马到成功,获得自己梦寐以求的岗位,成为众多求职人员中的佼佼者。

全书分为四单元,分别针对面试前准备部分、面试中初试部分、面试中复试部分及面试中终审部分进行相关的讲解。充分发挥学生的主体作用,为航空服务类专业学生提供体验完整航空公司英语面试环节的机会,激发学生兴趣,提高学生的面试通过率。本书适用的主要有中、高职院校空中乘务、航空服务、旅游英语等相近相关专业,也可供对民航职业充满热情并有志于投身此行业的其他人员参考。

本书由天津交通职业学院黄晨主编,负责组织全书的编写工作,包括结构设计、统稿、定稿等工作。具体编写分工如下:第一单元、第四单元主要由黄晨负责统筹编写;第二单元、第三单元的家庭情况、教育背景部分,由天津交通职业学院李响负责统筹编写;第三单元的品德个性、兴趣爱好、职业规划部分,由天津交通职业学院邱景翎负责统筹编写。

本书出现的姓名、学校、荣誉证书、航空公司等信息,仅供参考,特此说明。

本书是编者多年教学经验的总结,绝大部分内容为原创,少量内容在参考国内外一些著作的基础上进行了独立的挑选、编排、修改和创新,在此,编者特向有关作者和编辑表示最诚挚的谢意。编者水平有限,不足之处,欢迎广大读者批评指正!

编者

2018 年 12 月

CONTENTS 目录

Unit 1 如何写好求职简历——赢得面试机会

Unit 2 如何进行自我介绍——取得良好开端

Unit 3 如何巧答面试难题——博得评委青睐

Unit 4　如何应对专业问答——展现技能水平

Unit 4

Unit 1
如何写好求职简历——
赢得面试机会

Part I Introduction

简历是求职者向招聘单位表明其拥有能够满足特定工作要求的技能、态度和资质的专用文书。对应聘者来说，简历就是一种营销武器，是求职的敲门砖，能证明你拥有招聘方所需要的解决某类特定需求的能力，能促使你成功地得到面试的机会。

书写简历可以称为人生的第一份工作，对它投入有效时间的多少，往往意味着对工作的重视程度。在当今世界的求职市场上，所有雇主在招聘、选用人才时，首先就要看求职简历。可见，写好一份求职简历是求职成功的关键。

现如今，不仅是国外的航空公司，国内的很多民航企业，在招聘时都需要求职者同时寄送或者递交英文简历。由此可见，英文简历已经成为当前求职时必不可少的资料。

英文简历指的是用英语来介绍自己的个人资料，包括学历、工作经历、能力、业绩、性格、业余爱好等。准备好简历，犹如在战场上建起武器库，因为一份好的英文简历，不仅可以反映出你的个人综合实力，还能说明你的英语水平，所以，写好英文求职简历是求职时的头等大事，万万不可掉以轻心。

通常，一份完整的英文简历，应包括以下各项内容。

一、个人资料

1. 姓名

出生在说英语国家的人名的习惯写法是，名在前，姓在后。而中国人的姓名一般按汉语习惯书写，先姓后名。

2. 通信地址

英语通信地址的写法与汉语不同。英语是按从小到大的顺序写，汉语是按从大到小的顺序写。

3. 联系方式

联系方式包括手机号码、传真、电子邮箱等。

4. 出生日期

英文出生日期的写法与中文顺序不同，出生的月份和日期放在前面，年份放在后面。

5. 身高体重

在大部分航空公司的应聘表上，身高体重都属于必填项。

6. 业余爱好

针对面试岗位的不同，业余爱好的描写应有所侧重。例如：面试岗位为安全员的男生，应针对岗位技能需求，侧重描写自己体育方面的特长；面试岗位为乘务员的女生，应针对航空公司多才多艺的需求，侧重描写自己文艺等方面的专长。

这部分可在个人资料中简单写，也可作为一个单独模块，在简历后面突出描写。

7．政治面貌

如果你在学生阶段就是中国共产党党员，不要忘记着重强调这一点。对于航空公司来说，这意味着你比其他人更优秀，意味着你拥有能够在众多人中脱颖而出的能力。所以，对于面试是很有帮助的。

二、应聘职位

有时候，企业会同时招聘多种岗位的人才，简历中应当注明应聘职位，让招聘者一目了然。

三、学历

书写学历的顺序，应该从最高学历开始往下写。如果学历学位较高，则不必再写出中学与小学的学历。

四、工作经历

如果你是一名在职者，一般来说，目前的工作写在最前面，以前的经历依次写在后面。但是，如果在以往的工作经历中，有和现在应聘岗位存在相关性的经历，或者有需要重点突出的工作经历，应当先写，且应描述得更加详细。

如果你是在校学生，应着重强调可以突出企业所需能力的社会实践经历。例如：在面试航空公司乘务员岗位时，应将可以突出个人沟通能力及志愿者服务精神的经历写在最前面，然后，按照关联性的大小依次向后排序描写，不相关的可以写在最后面，或者省去。

五、职业技能

职业技能包括获得的职业资格证书名称、获得时间和等级水平。另外，还应描述与应聘工作岗位密不可分的技能，如电脑操作技能、语言能力等。

为了能够引起招聘者的足够注意，首先，英语简历必须突出自身的亮点，充分体现自己的优点与长处，对招聘单位而言，重要的资料要先写出来，如实具体地列出你与应聘职位相关的业绩和成果。其次，必须用简洁的语言来表达个人简历，最好字斟句酌，不要读起来令人生厌。另外，简历中要写出你在校园里参加的各种课外活动，尤其是志愿者服务，可以让企业面试官了解你的才能、修养和健康状态。

Part II Glossary

New Words	
disposal	*n.* 处理；支配；清理；安排
procedure	*n.* 程序，手续；步骤
etiquette	*n.* 礼节，礼仪；规矩

New Words	
ethics	n. 道德标准；伦理学；伦理观
nutrition	n. 营养，营养学；营养品
sanitation	n. 环境卫生；卫生设备；下水道设施
psychological	adj. 心理的；心理学的；精神上的
archives	n. 档案馆；档案文件
academic	adj. 学术的；理论的；学院的
league	n. 联盟；社团；范畴
outstanding	adj. 杰出的；显著的
contest	n. 竞赛；争夺；争论
competition	n. 竞争；比赛，竞赛
scholarship	n. 奖学金；学识，学问
obtain	vt. 获得
honorable	adj. 光荣的；可敬的
champion	n. 冠军
provincial	adj. 省的；地方性的
shortlisted	adj. 筛选后的
qualification	n. 资格；条件；限制；赋予资格
exposition	n. 博览会；阐述；展览会
technician	n. 技师，技术员；技巧纯熟的人
proficiency	n. 精通，熟练
license	n. 执照，许可证；特许
appraise	v. 鉴定；估价；评价
certificate	n. 证书；执照，文凭
fluent	adj. 流畅的，流利的；液态的
Mandarin	n.（中国）普通话
Cantonese	n. 粤语；广东话
dialect	n. 方言
fulltime	adj. 全职的

续表

New Words	
waitress	*n.* 女服务员；女侍者
clerk	*n.* 职员，办事员
Useful Phrases	
having a good command of	精通；对……掌握熟练
in charge of	管理；照料；负责

Part III   Useful Expressions

Stating Your Educational Background

Cabin Service 客舱服务
Hotel Management 酒店管理
Secretary 秘书
Basic Computer 计算机基础
Physics 物理
Composition 写作
Phonetics 语音学
Psychology 心理学
Public relations 公共关系
Emergency Equipment and Disposal of the Training 应急设备与处置训练
Cabin Service Procedures and Training 客舱服务程序训练
Announcement 广播词
Cabin English 客舱英语
Guiding Methods and Techniques 导游方法与技巧
Tourism Culture and Etiquette 旅游文化与礼仪
Tourist Psychology 旅游心理学
Tourist Cultures 旅游文化
Tourist Etiquette Science 旅游礼仪学
Vocational Ethics of Tourism 旅游职业道德
Hotel Management Principles 酒店管理原理
Hotel Marketing 酒店市场营销学
Accounting Principles 会计学原理
Front Service Management 前台服务管理

Housekeeping 客房管理

Food and Beverage Management 餐饮管理

Nutrition and Sanitation 营养与卫生

Hotel English 酒店英语

Business English 商务英语

Principles of Management 管理学原理

Business Communication 商务交际

Human Relations 人际关系

Secretarial Principles 秘书原理

Secretarial Practice 秘书实务

Office Automation 办公室自动化

Applied Writing for Secretarial 秘书应用写作

Secretarial English 文秘英语

Psychological Basics for Secretaries 秘书心理基础

Archives Administration 档案管理

Office Administration 办公室管理

Typing 打字

Shorthand 速记

1. I have completed a lot of courses concerning …, such as …, … and …, etc.
   我修过很多有关……的课程，例如……，……，……，等等。

2. The courses I took are as follows …, etc. My favorite courses are …
   我修过的课程包括……，等等。我最喜欢的课程有……

3. I also have studied some basic courses, such as …, etc.
   我还学了一些基础课程，例如……，等等。

4. Courses completed: …, 90; …, 95.
   所修课程：……，90 分；……，95 分。

5. As a major of hotel management …, I've taken such main courses as follows: …, …, and so on.
   作为酒店管理专业的学生，我修的课程主要有：……，……等。

6. Academic preparation for … : …
   大学时为……所做的学业准备：……

7. Majored in …. Courses covered are as follows: …, …, etc.
   ……专业。涉及的课程有如下几门：……，……等。

Stating Your Awards and Honors

Excellent League Member 优秀团员

Excellent Leader 优秀干部

Three Goods Outstanding Student 三好学生

Excellent Leader Of The University Student Council 校学生会优秀干部

English Speech Contest 英语演讲比赛

English Speaking Contest 英语口语大赛

Etiquette Competition 礼仪大赛

Professional Technique Competition 职业技能大赛

Career Planning Contest 职业规划大赛

(Network) Singer Competition（网络）歌手大赛

Sports Meeting 体育运动会

1. Got / Won / Obtained scholarship from the university / department in 2017.
   于 2017 年获得校级 / 系级奖学金。

2. Got / Won / Obtained the honorable title of … in 2017.
   于 2017 年荣获……的光荣称号。

3. Got / Won / Obtained the champion / runner-up in the final Competition of … held by ... in 2017.
   于 2017 年获得……举办的……总决赛的冠军 / 亚军。

4. Got / Won / Obtained the first / second / third prize of the National / Provincial / City Competition of … in 2017.
   于 2017 年获得全国 / 全省 / 全市……大赛一等奖 / 二等奖 / 三等奖。

5. Got / Won / Obtained the first / second / third place in … contest / competition in 2017.
   于 2017 年获得……比赛第一 / 二 / 三名。

6. Has been shortlisted for the top 10 / 100 in the National / Provincial / City Competition of … by College Students.
   曾在全国 / 全省 / 全市大学生……大赛中入围十 / 百强。

Stating Your Occupational Qualifications

Business Secretary 商务秘书

International Business Secretary 国际商务秘书

Tour Guide's Qualification 导游资格

Assistant Exposition Technician 助理会展商务师

Computer Hi-Tech Office Software 高新技术办公软件资格

Computer Operator's Qualification 计算机操作员资格

National Computer Rank Examination 全国计算机等级考试

International Certified Chinese Teacher Qualification 国际汉语教师资格

JLPT (Japanese Language Proficiency Test) 日语能力测试

Driving License 驾照

Appraising Secretary Qualification 秘书技能鉴定

Appraising Foreign Oriented Secretary Qualification 涉外秘书技能鉴定

Appraising Public Relations Officer Qualification 公关人员技能鉴定

1. Got / Received / Obtained a Certificate of … in 2017.
   于 2017 年获得……证书。
2. Got / Received / Obtained a … Qualification Certificate in 2017.
   于 2017 年获得……资格证书。
3. Got / Received / Obtained Grade Two Certificate of … in 2017.
   于 2017 年获得……二级证书。
4. Got / Received / Obtained the first / second / third / fourth / fifth grade of appraising …
   Qualification in 2017.
   于 2017 年获得……技能鉴定一级 / 二级 / 三级 / 四级 / 五级。
5. Got / Received / Obtained a certificate of … Qualification issued by … in 2017.
   于 2017 年获得由……颁发的……证书。

Stating Your Language Abilities

English

Band Four / Six of CET (College English Test) 大学英语 4 级 / 6 级

Band Four / Five / Six of PETS (Public English Test System) 全国公共英语考试 4 级 / 5 级 / 6 级

Band Four / Eight of TEM (Test for English Majors) 英语专业 4 级 / 8 级

BEC (Business English Certificate) 商务英语考试

TOEIC (Test Of English for International Communication) 托业

IELTS (International English Language Testing System) 雅思

TOEFL (Test Of English as a Foreign Language) 托福

GRE (Graduate Record Examination) 美国研究生入学考试

TSE (Test of Spoken English) 英语口语测试

1. Passed ….
   通过了……
2. My marks for … : … points.
   我的……考试的得分是……
3. Did well in ….
   在……测试中表现出色。
4. Fluent in English ….
   在英语的……方面流利。
5. Having a good command of English in ….
   精通……英语。
6. Good at English for ….
   擅长……英语。
7. Proficient in … English.
   擅长……英语。

Others

1. Got Band 1A / Band 1B / Band 2A / Band 2B / Band 3A / Band 3B of Mandarin Level Test (Putonghua Test).
   获得普通话测试的等级为一级甲等 / 一级乙等 / 二级甲等 / 二级乙等 / 三级甲等 / 三级乙等。

2. Language: Mandarin, Cantonese, English.
   语言：普通话、粤语、英语。

3. Able to speak … Dialect.
   会说……方言。

Stating Your Computer Skills

1. Passed Rank One / Two / Three / Four of NCRE (National Computer Rank Examination).
   通过全国计算机等级考试的一级 / 二级 / 三级 / 四级。

2. Having a good command of such word processing software as Word and WPS.
   熟悉 Word 和 WPS 文字处理软件。

3. Proficiency in Office software.
   熟练操作办公软件。

4. Proficient in the use of Office software such as Word and PPT.
   熟练使用 Word、PPT 等办公软件。

Stating Your Work Experiences

… Clothes Store ……服装店

… Restaurant ……餐厅

… Hotel ……酒店

… Group Corporation Ltd. ……集团有限公司

public relations manager 公关经理

sales 售货员

shopping guide 导购员

tour guide 导游

receiving visitors 接待访客

scheduling meeting 安排会议

1. Practical summer experience.
   暑假的实践经历。

2. Fulltime in summers, part time during college.
   暑假全职，上课时间兼职。

3. Responsibilities: …, …and…
   工作职责：……，……和……

4. Employed at … as waitress, 2016.

2016 年，在……当服务员。

5. Worked 18 hours weekly as a … at the … of ….

在……当一名……，每周工作 18 小时。

6. Clerked in … , in charge of …, 2016.

2016 年，在……当店员，负责…… 工作。

Part IV　Instances

例 1：

RESUME

Name: × × ×

Phone: × × ×　　　　　　　　　　　　E-mail: × × ×

Career Objective: Flight Attendant

Highlights:

Excellent in singing and presentation.

Awarded as × × × in × × × competition.

Personal Information

Gender: Female　　　　　　　　　　Age: 21 (born in Sept. 8, 1994)

Height: 168 cm　　　　　　　　　　Weight: 55 kg

Place of Birth: Tianjin　　　　　　　Marital Status: Single

Education & Training

2017.9-2017.11　　　　　　　　　Beijing Aviation Training Center

　　　　　　　　　　　　　　　　Junior Flight Attendant Training

Certificate: Certificate of Junior Flight Attendant

I finished the following professional courses excellently:

IATA Passenger Fares and Ticketing.

IATA Basic Cargo Skills and Procedures.

Etiquette.

Aviation Services-related Skills, such as Customer Service, etc.

2013.7-2017.9　　　　　　　　　　The University of × × × ×

Major: In-flight service

Certificate: ×××

I finished the following courses with excellent grades:

English.

Aviation Transportation.

Japanese on Cabin Service.

Computer Literate

Excellent computer & Internet skills.

Good at using Microsoft Office, Adobe Photoshop, Network skills, etc.

例 1：

简　历

姓名：×××

电话：×××　　　　　　　　　　　　邮箱：×××

求职目标：民航乘务员

个人亮点：

擅长唱歌、演讲；

曾经获得 ××× 比赛 ××× 奖。

个人信息

性别：女　　　　　　　　　　　　年龄：21（1994 年 9 月 8 日生）

身高：168 cm　　　　　　　　　　体重：55 kg

出生地：天津　　　　　　　　　　婚姻状况：单身

教育与培训

2017 年 9 月至 2017 年 11 月　　　北京航空培训中心

初级乘务员培训

获得证书：初级乘务员证书

我出色地完成了以下专业课程的学习：

IATA 航空客运服务。

IATA 航空货运服务。

服务礼仪。

航空服务相关技能等。

2013 年 7 月至 2017 年 9 月　　　　×××× 大学

专业：空中乘务

获得证书：×××

我以优异成绩完成了以下课程：

英语；

航空运输；

乘务日语。

计算机水平

能够熟练运用计算机及互联网处理各类与专业相关的事务。

熟练使用 Microsoft Office, Adobe Photoshop 等应用软件，能够熟练应用互联网、电子软件等常规信息技术。

例 2 ：

A RESUME of × × × (Name)

Personal Information

Birth Date: November 19, 1996

Birth Place: Beijing

Political Status: League Member

Gender: Female

Height: 167 cm

Weight: 51 kg

Phone: × × ×

E-mail: × × ×

Position Wanted

Flight Attendant

Employment History

| 1 / 2018-Present | Receptionist, Beijing Hotel |
| 8 / 2017-12 / 2017 | Office Clerk; Beijing Dingdong Century Co. |

Educational Background

| 9 / 2014-7 / 2017 | Specialized in Cabin Service at × × × |
| | Courses taken: × × ×, × × × … |

Language Ability

Standard Mandarin and fluent English.

Personal Interests

Listening to classical music and reading books.

Honors

Excellent League Member

例 2：

×××（姓名）的个人简历

个人资料

出生日期：1996 年 11 月 19 日

出生地：北京

政治面貌：团员

性别：女

身高：167 cm

体重：51 kg

电话：×××

邮箱：×××

求职意向

乘务员

工作经历

2018 年 1 月至今	前台，北京饭店
2017 年 8 月至 2017 年 12 月	办公室文员，北京叮咚世纪有限公司

教育背景

2014 年 9 月至 2017 年 7 月	×××大学空中乘务专业
	所修课程：×××，×××……

语言能力

普通话标准、英语流利。

个人兴趣

听古典音乐、读书。

所获荣誉

优秀团员。

Part V Tips

求职简历的"三要五不要"

1. 三要

（1）要简洁直白。很多求职者为了使自己的简历看起来与众不同，往往使用过多的形容词和修饰语。其实，过于华丽的语言，并不适合放在求职简历中。尤其是英文简历，复杂的句子结构，并不常见的单词，不仅会使面试官一头雾水，而且，简单的语法错误，还会给航空公司留下不好的印象。

（2）要表述清晰。在航空公司应聘时，对个人情况的介绍要非常详细，姓名、性别、出生年月、政治面貌、身高、体重、电话和应聘职位，这些都是必需的。有的应聘者由于害羞或将身高体重视为个人隐私，认为不便向外透露，这样便会使面试官不能更好地判断你是否符合该航空公司的标准，所以，不利于应聘的成功。

（3）要避谈薪资。很多求职者对于是否应该在求职简历中标注自己的薪资要求存在疑惑，人力资源经理都认为，简历上写上对工资的要求要冒很大的风险，最好不写。对于刚出校门的大学生来说，第一份工作的薪水并不重要，不要在这方面费太多脑筋。

2．五不要

（1）不要太长。目前，求职者在撰写简历时，总是希望可以更全面地展示自己的优点，所以容易造成内容普遍过长的现象。其实，简历内容过多，反而会淹没一些有价值的闪光点。每当到了招聘季，由于应聘者过多，每家航空公司尤其是大型的认可度较高的航空公司，都会收到堆积如山的简历，工作人员不可能每一份都仔细研读，一份简历通常只用一分钟就看完了，再长的简历也超不过三分钟。所以，简历尽量要短，只要一页纸就足够了。

另外，简历中不需要附带成绩单或荣誉证书等佐证材料，如果航空公司对你感兴趣，自然会要求求职者在面试时带去，所以，只需在简历上列出这些就可以了。

（2）不要弄虚作假。面试官对于应聘者的第一印象便来自于求职简历，所以，求职者要按照实际情况填写，不要含有水分，一定要真实客观。任何虚假的内容都要避免，不要虚张声势，否则，容易给面试官留下十分不好的印象。即使有的人靠含有水分的简历得到了复试的机会，但后期也会露出马脚，千万不要踩这根红线。对于不诚信的人，任何航空公司的答案都将会是NO！

（3）不要过分谦虚。简历要求内容全面，但不代表就要把自己的一切都表达出来，尤其是弱项。如果在简历中特别注明自己某项能力不强，这就是过分谦虚了。实际上，不写这些并不代表说假话。

（4）不要出现低级错误。企业最不能容忍的事情，就是简历上出现低级错误，或者排版上有技术性错误，或者被折叠得皱皱巴巴，或者是有污点。尤其是一份英文简历，有的应聘者故意使用不常见的单词或修饰语，以展示自己的英文水平。但是，有时候一个字母打错，单词的意思则会完全不同。再加上未经检查就打印出来递送给面试官，航空公司会认为，你是一个不踏实、不用心的人，如果连求职都这样，那么未来工作也不会用心。

（5）不要追求花哨。现在的简历都讲究包装，要精致、华丽、与众不同，甚至有的连纸都是五颜六色的。其实，面试航空公司等民航类企业的服务岗位时，简历并不需要做得太花哨，用质量较好的白色 A4 纸打印即可。另外，也没有必要制作封面，这样做反而会增加简历的厚度，给企业造成负担。

Part VI Supplementary Reading

A: How to avoid such things？

On the flight from Hangzhou to Xiamen, flight attendants were talking about how to distribute the rest of the newspapers properly because of the shortage. Just then, a little boy asked from the back "Aunt, I need a piece of newspaper." The stewardess found out that he was just a child, said half-jokingly "You can't have it. You cannot read newspapers." The little boy said "I can understand, I know!" The stewardess then smiled, and went on distributing the newspapers. A man's voice came from the side "My son bought the adult ticket but got far less service. I need an explanation!" Shocked at the sudden sound, the stewardess felt very ashamed and immediately went to apologize to the passenger. Finally, he forgave her and didn't complain in the end.

Language is one of the important criteria of a tourist's evaluation on the service quality. In the service process, proper, clear, pure and sweet language will make passengers have a pleasant warm feeling and have a good impression of the service; on the other hand, if the language is "bad", hard or abrupt, it will be difficult for passengers to accept. Strong language stimulation can cause dissatisfaction and complaints of passengers. Airlines will be seriously affected in the credibility of the company. In this case, it isn't proper for a flight attendant to say like that. During the execution of the flight task, each passenger should be treated fairly. The flight attendants should pay attention to their own languages, especially those to children. In addition, the newspaper should be justly distributed to maximize the shortage problems during the flight.

B: Why should an international flights have duty-free service？

Korean Air was the first airline with duty-free exhibition area in A380. It will show a variety of duty-free goods, including alcohol, cosmetics, perfume and other kinds of fashion accessories. It also arranges some full-time flight attendants in the duty-free demonstration area, who are responsible for providing suggestions and answering questions for passengers on all kinds of duty-free goods during the whole flight. A passenger said "With this new way of duty-free sales, everyone will be able to get items they want easily."

Many airlines have their own duty-free service, which is a significant air service project.

First of all, it is convenient for passengers and enriches their journey. After boarding, the passenger can read the duty-free shopping guide book in the seat pocket in front of them, shop easily and leisurely. The airline offers a variety of payment methods, such as cash, credit card, etc., so the duty-free goods service is welcomed by the passengers because it is convenient and fast.

Secondly, the good conduct of duty-free sales service on the plane does not only strengthen the communication between the crew and passengers, but also create a good economic benefit.

Thirdly, the duty-free goods service can build airline brands, maintain the relationship with passengers and improve the satisfaction.

C: How to assist the elder passengers to get off the plane with their baggage properly?

A flight stopped in Xi'an. Two elder people asked attendant Wang come and help with their luggage. Wang was just about to help. A man came over with a box, shouting "Excuse me! Pardon me!" Wang quickly asked the elder people step inside for their safety. After that, the passengers stepped off the aircraft one after another. The old lady was angry at being kept waiting so long. She let her husband take down the bag. "You did't help us with our baggage even I asked you to?" she said grumpily, "Your service is really bad!" Wang were shocked and felt aggrieved at this sort of thing. But the elder passengers had already gone away when he tried to explain.

In this case, Wang played a passive role in the relationship. He had not been able to control the situation. As a matter of fact, he was upset at being criticized for no reason. The attendant should be concerned with the elder passengers during descent. Go and ask the elders. What is the number of the luggage? Is there anybody accompanying? Is there anybody meeting at the airport? Do they need help? Greet them and comfort them. When it is time to get off the plane, flight attendants should assist the elder with their luggage actively. If there are some passengers who want to pass, he/she (the attendant) could negotiate with them, "Excuse me, would you please wait for a few minutes and let the elder go first?" And then send the elder to the cabin door. If there is too much luggage, then you should contact the ground staff.

Unit 2
如何进行自我介绍——取得良好开端

Part I Introduction

一、面试时进行自我介绍包含四方面

1. 我是谁

自我介绍的第一步是要让面试官知道你是谁。在这一步，你主要介绍自己的个人履历和专业特长，包括姓名、年龄、籍贯等个人基本信息，教育背景以及与应聘职位密切相关的特长等。生动、形象、个性化地介绍自己的姓名，不仅能够引起面试官的注意，而且可以使面试的氛围变得轻松。个性化地介绍姓名有多种方式，你可以从名字的音、义、形或者从名字的来历进行演绎。

例如：从名字的音：我叫邵飞，谐音少非，希望生活能少一点是是非非。从名字的义：我叫俞非鱼。古语有言：子非鱼安知鱼之乐。父母亲希望我过得像鱼儿一般自在逍遥。从名字的形：我叫陈赟。我的父亲叫陈斌，斌的宝贝就是赟。从名字的来历：我叫赵丹，赵本山的赵，宋丹丹的丹。父母希望我能够像他们一样幽默地对待生活。

2. 我做过什么

做过什么，代表着你的经验和经历。在这个部分，你主要介绍与应聘职位密切相关的实践经历，包括校内活动经历、相关的兼职和实习经历、社会实践等。你要说清楚确切的时间、地点、担任的职务、工作内容等，这样让面试官觉得真实、可信。特别需要注意的是，你的经历可能很多，你不可能面面俱到，那些与应聘职位无关的内容，即使你引以为荣也要忍痛舍弃。

3. 我做成过什么

做成过什么，代表着你的能力和水平。在这部分，你主要介绍与应聘职位所需能力相关的个人业绩，包括校内活动成果和校外实践成果。介绍个人业绩，就是摆成绩，把自己在不同阶段做成的有代表性的事情介绍清楚。

你在介绍个人业绩时，需要注意以下方面。

（1）业绩要与应聘职位需要的能力紧密相关。例如，如果你应聘文员，就不需要介绍销售业绩。

（2）介绍"你自己"的业绩，而不是团队业绩，因为用人单位要招聘的是"你"，而不是"你们"。

（3）业绩要有量化的数字，要有具体的证据。不要用笼统的"很好""很多"，也不要用"大概""约""基本"等概数，而要用确切的数字。例如：我一周内卖出了34箱方便面。

（4）介绍的内容应当有所侧重，不要说流水账，要着重介绍那些能体现自己能力的重点。

（5）介绍业绩取得的具体过程时，要巧妙地埋伏笔。例如：在介绍校外实践成果时，你可以这样描述："在工作中遇到了很多的问题，不过我还是成功地克服并达成了业务目标。"引导面试官提问"遇到了哪些问题"，然后你就可以进一步阐述细节内容，体现出自己处理问题的能力。

4. 我想做什么

想做什么，代表着你的职业理想。在这个部分，你应该介绍自己对应聘职位、行业的看法和理想，包括你的职业生涯规划、对工作的兴趣与热情、未来的工作蓝图、对行业发展趋势的看法等。在介绍时，你还要针对应聘职位合理编排每部分的内容。与应聘职位关系越密切的内容，介绍的次序越靠前，介绍得越详细。

你在自我介绍时，还应该避开介绍内容的禁忌——忌讳主动介绍个人爱好。忌讳使用过多的"我"字眼。忌讳头重脚轻。忌讳介绍背景而不介绍自己。忌讳夸口。忌讳说谎。忌讳过于简单，没有内容。

二、自我介绍的时间要恰到好处

1. 三分钟自我介绍

如果面试官没有特别强调，那么自我介绍的时间3分钟最合适。你可以根据自我介绍的四部分内容，这样分配时间：第一分钟主要介绍自己的姓名、年龄、学历、专业特长、实践经历等；第二分钟主要介绍个人业绩，应届毕业生可着重介绍相关的在校活动和社会实践的成果；第三分钟可谈谈对应聘职位的理想和对本行业的看法。

通常情况下，每分钟180～200字的语速是比较合适的。这样的语速可以让对方感到舒服，同时也能更加有效地传递信息，增加面试官对你的印象分。

2. 一分钟自我介绍

有时候，面试官会规定自我介绍的时间，你应该怎样应对呢？面试官规定的自我介绍时间缩短，如"做一个1分钟的自我介绍"。遇到这种情况，你可以精选事先准备的3分钟自我介绍内容，突出"做成过什么"，展现你与应聘职位相关的能力。

自我介绍要考察的内容：首先要搞清楚为什么面试官要请你做自我介绍？面试官通过自我介绍想考察被面试者什么？只有了解面试官的目的，被面试者才能做好自我介绍。

面试官通过被面试者自我介绍要考察以下五方面内容。

第一，考察自我介绍内容和递交简历内容是否相冲突？如果简历是真实的，口述自我介绍就不会有明显出入。如果简历有假，自我介绍阶段一般就会露马脚。如面试官提问时，被面试者回答"我的经历在简历里都写了"，面试官会认为这人嘚瑟，印象分一下子降为负数。

第二，考察被面试者基本的逻辑思维能力、语言表达能力，总结提炼概括能力。

第三，考察被面试者是否聚焦，是否简练和精干，现场的感知能力与把控能力。

第四，考察被面试者初步的自我认知能力和价值取向。因为被面试者要叙述职业切换关键节点处的原因，尤其要考察最近职业变动的原因。

第五，考察被面试者是否听明白了面试官的话以及时间的掌控能力。有时面试官给出的问题是"请您用3～5分钟做一自我介绍"，被面试者有时一介绍就超过10分钟，甚至20分钟，逼得面试官不得不多次提醒引导。

所以说，自我介绍是被面试者在纸面之外最能够呈现能力的一个地方。一般情况下，也是被面试者在整个面试过程中唯一一次主动展示自我的机会。如果还有一次，那就是面试官最后一个问题："您还有什么问我的？"但这个问题通常只是面试官认为被面试者基本靠谱了，才会留下这个问题。

Part II　Glossary

New Words	
raise	*n.* 高地；上升；加薪
performance	*n.* 性能；绩效；表演
honor	*n.* 荣誉；信用；头衔
opportunity	*n.* 时机，机会
advertise	*vi.* 做广告，登广告
advertisement	*n.* 广告，宣传
position	*n.* 位置，方位；职位
vacation	*vi.* 休假，度假
anxious	*adj.* 焦虑的；担忧的
bachelor	*n.* 学士；单身汉
acquire	*vt.* 获得；取得；学到
draw	*vt.* 画；拉；吸引
degree	*n.* 程度，等级；度
independent	*adj.* 独立的；单独的；无党派的；不受约束的
easy-going	*adj.* 随和的，容易相处的
congenial	*adj.* 适意的；一致的
choir	*vt.* 合唱
widespread	*adj.* 普遍的，广泛的；分布广的
optimistic	*adj.* 乐观的
honest	*adj.* 诚实的，实在的；可靠的
modest	*adj.* 谦虚的，谦逊的；适度的
fluent	*adj.* 流畅的，流利的；液态的
fairly	*adv.* 相当地；公平地；简直
authentic	*adj.* 真正的，真实的；可信的
volunteer	*n.* 志愿者
command	*n.* 指挥，控制；命令；司令部

New Words	
version	*n.* 版本；译文；倒转术
asset	*n.* 资产；优点；有用的东西
accomplishment	*n.* 成就；完成；技艺，技能
ambition	*n.* 野心，雄心；抱负，志向
positive	*n.* 正数；正片
diligently	*adv.* 勤奋地；勤勉地
supervision	*n.* 监督，管理
Useful Phrases	
settle down	安定下来
apply for	申请
get along with	与……相处
allow sb. to do sth.	允许某人做某事

Part III Useful Expressions

Opening Speech

1. Let me introduce myself. / Let me do some introduction.
   让我来介绍一下自己。

2. Which aspect do you want to know about me?
   您想知道我哪方面的情况？

3. What do you want to know about myself?
   您想了解我什么？

4. Good morning / afternoon / evening, my name is .... It is really a great honor to have this opportunity / chance to introduce myself. I would like to answer whatever you may raise, and I hope I can make a good performance today.
   上午好 / 下午好 / 晚上好！我的名字叫……很荣幸能有这个机会进行自我介绍。我乐意回答你们所提出来的任何问题。我希望我今天能表现得非常出色。

5. Good morning! It is really my honor to have this opportunity for an interview, and I hope I can make a good performance today.
   早上好，很荣幸有这个面试的机会，希望我今天能表现得非常出色。

Position Applied

1. I noticed that you advertised a job in ××× paper.
   我看到你们在 ××× 报纸上刊登的招聘广告。

2. I'm coming for your advertisement for ....
   我是来应聘你们广告上的……职位的。

3. I have applied for the position of ....
   我申请了贵公司的……职位。

4. I haven't done anything like that before.
   我以前没有做过这种工作。

5. I think I'm quite fit for ×××.
   我觉得我很适合做 ××× 工作。

6. I want a job with a vacation every year.
   我想找一个每年都有假期的工作。

7. I'm 18 years old and will be graduating soon.
   我今年 18 岁，不久即可毕业。

8. I am 20 years old and hope to find a company to settle down.
   我今年 20 岁，希望能找到一个公司，以便安定下来。

9. Since my graduation from the school two years ago, I have been employed in ××× as a ×××.
   自从两年前从学校毕业后，我就一直在 ××× 单位 ××× 岗位工作。

Personal Information

1. I am...years old, born in...province / Beijing, northeast / southeast / southwest...of China, and I am currently a freshman（大一新生）/ sophomore（大二学生）/ junior（大三学生）/ senior（大四学生）student at ××× Institute of ×××.
   我今年……岁，出生在……省 / 北京，它位于中国的东北 / 东南 / 西南……部。我目前是 ××× 学院大一 / 大二 / 大三 / 大四的学生。

2. My major is ×××. I'll get a bachelor degree after graduation.
   我主修 ××× 专业。在我毕业以后，我将会获得学士学位。

3. In the past 1 / 2 / 3 years, I spend most of my time on study. I have passed CET Band 4 / 6 and I have acquired basic knowledge of ××× both in theory and in practice.
   在过去的 1 / 2 / 3 年中，我把大量的时间用在学习上。我已经通过了大学英语 4 / 6 级等级考试，掌握了 ××× 专业理论和实践方面的基础知识。

4. I got my bachelor degree in Literature.
   我获得了文学学士学位。

5. I have lots of interests, such as singing, dancing, drawing and so on.
   我有很多兴趣爱好，如唱歌、跳舞、画画等。

6. I'm ××× and I am 26 years old. I come from Beijing, and I have just got my master degree

from × × × University. I have been studying × × × for 3 years and I think it is fun.

我叫×××，今年 26 岁。我来自北京，刚从×××大学获得硕士学位。我学习×××已经有三个年头，我觉得这门学科非常有意思。

7. I am the only child in my family, but I am very independent.

我虽然是独生子女，但是我是很独立的。

8. My family consists of my father, mother, brother and me.

我们家由爸爸、妈妈、弟弟和我组成。

Hobbies and Character

1. I am easy-going and congenial, with a strong sense of responsibility and good team-spirit.

我为人谦和友善，做事态度认真，有强烈的责任感和良好的团队精神。

2. I love travelling very much.

我特别喜欢旅行。

3. I have played a couple of important roles in the student organizations, honing the interpersonal communication skills and organizational capability.

我曾担任学校社团职务，培养了良好的人际交往技巧与组织能力。

4. I have a wide range of hobbies, including oral English, music, movies and literature.

我兴趣广泛，喜爱英语口语、音乐、影视以及文学。

5. I am a member of the choir in our school.

我是学校合唱团的成员。

6. I have studied ballet for more than eight years.

我学过八年的芭蕾舞了。

7. I can't imagine how my life would be if there is no music in my life.

我不敢想象如果我的生命里没有音乐会怎么样。

8. Being influenced by my family, I love music very much.

由于深受家庭的影响，我很喜欢音乐。

9. I am open-minded, quick in thought and fond of history. In my spare time, I have broad interests like reading books, especially books related to historical events.

我的性格很开朗，反应灵敏，并且喜欢历史。在空闲时间，我有许多爱好，比如读书，尤其是有关于历史事件的书籍。

10. I am good at surfing online. My hobby is widespread, such as reading, listening to music, playing basketball.

我擅长网上冲浪。我爱好广泛，如阅读，听音乐，打篮球。

11. I am very optimistic and easy to get along with. I have many friends. Teamwork spirit is very important in this age. I think if we want to make big achievement, it's very important to learn how to cooperate with other people. My motto is "× × ×", so I always remind myself to be honest and modest to everyone .

我很乐观，很容易相处。我有很多朋友。在这个时代，团队合作精神是非常重要的。我认为，如果我们想取得重大的成就，学会如何与他人合作是非常重要的。我的座右铭是"×××"，所以我时刻提醒自己要诚实和谦逊地对待身边的人。

Capability and Accomplishment

1. I am fluent in oral English, with fairly good reading and writing ability, speaking authentic and mandarin-Chinese.

   我英语口语流利，具有良好的英语阅读、写作能力，普通话标准。

2. I have completed all the courses in the specialized field, obtaining good command of theoretic knowledge and experimental and DIY skill, very adaptable and good at learning.

   我已经顺利完成专业课程学习，熟练掌握专业理论知识和实验技能，具有很强的动手能力，善于学习新知识和适应新环境。

3. Besides, I have attended several sports meetings held in Beijing. I am also the volunteer of China Tennis Open, Chinese Badminton Masters.... Through these I have a deeply understanding of sports training.

   除此以外，我还参加了在北京举行的许多运动会。我还是中国网球公开赛，羽毛球大师赛……的志愿者。通过这些，我对一些运动训练有了一个更深刻的了解。

4. Good command of Computer skills: familiar with different versions of Windows OS and Office application software, able to program with C and FORTRAN languages, obtained some experience and understanding about other widely-used software like AutoCAD, Photoshop, CorelDRAW and Dreamweaver.

   具备良好的计算机技能，熟悉不同版本的 Windows 操作系统以及 Office 系列办公软件，可使用 C 语言和 FORTRAN 语言进行编程，对于 AutoCAD、Photoshop、CorelDRAW、Dreamweaver 也有一定的了解和使用经验。

5. I feel that my greatest strength is my ability to stick to things to get them done. I feel a real sense of accomplishment when I finish a job that turns out just as I planned. I've set some high goals for myself.

   我认为我最大的优点是能够执着地尽力把事情办好。当做完一件工作而其成果又正合我的预想时，我会有一种真正的成就感。我给自己定了一些高目标。

6. I am young, bright, energetic with strong study-ambition. I have good presentation skills and a positive active and mind.

   我年轻、聪明、精力充沛，并有很强的事业心。我有良好的表达能力和灵活的头脑。

7. I have a positive work attitude and be willing and able to work diligently without supervision。

   我有积极的工作态度，愿意和能够在没有监督的情况下勤奋地工作。

8. I have a hard-working spirit, excellent learning ability, ambition and good health.

   我具备吃苦耐劳的精神，学习能力优，事业心强和身体棒。

Part IV Instances

例 1：

Good morning everyone, my name is ×××. I am ×× years old. I graduated from ×××. I have a dream since I was a child. I dream that one day I can fly in the blue sky like the bird. Now I have the chance to make it come true. If I can take this job, I'll try my best to do everything well, because I love this job.

Thank you.

各位早上好，我的名字叫×××，我今年××岁，毕业于××学校。从小我就有一个梦想，梦想着有一天能像鸟儿一样在蓝天上飞翔。现在我终于有了这个机会来实现我儿时的梦想。如果我能得到这个工作，我会尽我的全力去做好它。因为我爱这份工作。谢谢。

例 2：

I'm very glad to join in the interview. First, let me introduce myself to you. My name is ×××, I'm 20 years old. I come from Zhejiang, and I'm an outgoing girl, I like philosophy and sport. I hope that I can do something for the Beijing Olympics. If you give me the great chance, I will not let you disappoint. I hope that you are satisfied with me, thank you!

很高兴能参加这次面试，首先让我做个自我介绍，我叫×××，今年21岁，来自浙江，曾经做过网管的工作，学到了很多东西。我是一个很活泼开朗的女孩，喜欢哲学和运动。我希望能为北京举办奥运会做点什么。如果贵公司给我这个机会，我想我不会让您失望的。希望我今天的表现能令您满意，谢谢！

例 3：

Good morning, ladies and gentleman, I'm currently in the second year of my study on aviation in a technical secondary school, major in flight attendant. I was born in a city of beauty and abundance, Chengdu. My hobbies are singing and dancing since my childhood. Besides that, I participated actively in inter-school model competitions as well as internships in hotels, which allows me to have the experience of the administration and management of a firm. Having a career in aviation services is my dream since my childhood, hence I'm eager to have a chance to work in your company.

各位好，我是来自航空中专的二年级学生，所学专业是空中乘务。我出生在美丽而又富饶的天府之国成都。唱歌跳舞是我从小以来的特长和爱好。另外，我积极地参与了我校模特队举办的各种比赛和活动，同时在酒店实习的经历也让我积累了公司行政及运营方面的经验。能进入航空公司工作是我儿时的梦想，所以我非常想成为贵公司的一员。

例 4：

I am a lively, cheerful and ambitious girl. I am 170cm tall and 54kg in weight. I like to treat everything around us with a smile. A friendly smile can pass a good intention to people. To be a stewardess is what I have always dream of, I like the feeling of flying in the blue sky. When facing difficulties, I never back down, I always smile to confront them and have the courage to move forward. I love to be a flight attendant. It is a noble profession. I have a positive and optimistic attitude and tradition of hard work. I believe I can do it. (I am an extroverted and aspirant girl. I am 1.7 meters tall and 54 kilograms. I like smile with all things around me for smile can give friendly message to others. Being a stewardess is my dream for I like the feeling of flying in the sky. I never give up facing difficulties. I always smile with them and keep forward. I love the job of being a stewardess. I have optimistic attitude and work hard. I believe that I am competent enough to suit/do the job.)

我是一个外向上进的女孩。身高 1.7 米，体重 54 千克。我喜欢对周围的一切微笑，因为微笑可以传递给别人友好的信息。成为一名空姐是我的梦想，因为我喜欢在天空中飞翔。面对困难，我从不放弃，总是微笑着继续前进。我喜欢空姐这份工作，我有积极乐观的态度，能够努力工作，我相信自己可以胜任这份工作。

例 5：

Good morning / Good afternoon, my name is Yang Haiyan and you can call me Yanzi. I like flying in the air like a swallow.

It is my honor to have this opportunity to participate in this interview, I would like to answer whatever you may raise, and I hope I can make a good performance today.

Now I will introduce myself briefly. I am 20 years old and was born in Jiangsu Province. I grew up in a sweet home which consists of my dad, mom, brother and me. I am an optimistic and confident girl. I have full confidence in a bright future, I believe I can do the best. Punctuality and diligence are the most important characters for me, I will try my best. Although I just graduated from school, I have confidence in my future.

Flying in the sky as an airline stewardess has been my dream since childhood. This is why I want to work in an airplane, why I am standing here for an interview. I hope my application will be granted, so I will put the dream of my best service all over the world, the Civil Aviation Administration of China I can come true a member.

All this. Nice talking to you. Thank you.

早上好 / 下午好，我叫杨海燕，你可以叫我燕子。我喜欢像燕子一样在空中飞翔的感觉。

很荣幸能有这个机会参加此次面试，我希望今天我能有好的表现。

现在我将简要地介绍一下自己。我今年 20 岁，出生在江苏省。我成长在一个甜蜜的家庭，有我的爸爸、妈妈、弟弟和我。我是一个乐观和自信的女孩。我对美好的未来充满信心，我相信我能做到最好。我将尽我最大的努力在未来的职业中做到守时和勤奋，这两点非常重要。虽然我刚从学校毕业，但我对未来充满信心。

在天空飞翔，成为空姐是我儿时的梦想。这就是为什么我渴望在飞机上工作，为什么我会站在这里的原因了。我希望我的申请能够被接受，我将竭尽全力为旅客提供最优质的服务，以此实现自己飞越世界的梦想。中国民航，请让我成为你正式的一员！

感谢您的倾听。

Part V Tips

一、自我介绍有哪些禁忌

1. 忌讳主动介绍个人爱好

面试时不要介绍个人爱好，除非面试官主动问。有被面试者虽然工作多年了，往往在做自我介绍时，仍兴致盎然地介绍个人爱好，如登山、打球、听音乐，等等，不仅白白浪费时间，还让面试官感觉你成熟度不够。注意，个人爱好不等于个人特长。

2. 忌讳头重脚轻

面试刚开始时，面试者把自己的经历说得天花乱坠，当发现时间不够用了，之后的介绍则只能草草了事，面试官会对你刚开始的讲述印象深刻而之后的内容则容易被忽略，也许会因此对你的能力判断产生误差。

3. 忌讳过于简单，没有内容

此类面试者很爽快，1分钟把工作经历全部说完，没有下文了，只介绍自己干了什么，没介绍干成了什么和自己的专业特长，全等着面试官发问。而面试官除了通过你的叙述简单了解了你的经历，其余什么也不知道，不知该从何问起。这就等于你放弃了一次主动展示自己的机会，等面试官发问你就得被动应付。面试官也会认为你过于轻率，或沟通表达能力不强。

4. 忌讳介绍背景而不介绍自己

面试者把自己对企业的了解介绍了很多，对自己的介绍很少。甚至有的已经是国内知名和国际知名企业，面试者还把企业的发展历程兴致勃勃地介绍了10分钟。这样面试官会认为你智商有问题，或不知道自己干什么来的。

5. 忌讳把岗位职责当个人业绩来呈现

比如应聘市场部总监岗位，结果面试者把整个市场部的职责逐条介绍了一遍，占了很多时间。其实，面试者应该介绍自己曾经在担任市场部总监时所做出的个人努力，采取的工作方法，动用了什么资源，最终取得的实实在在的业绩。出现这种情况，往往是面试经验不足造成的，通过专业的猎头顾问，会帮助面试者避免这种低级错误。

6. 忌讳说满和说谎

在做自我介绍时，全部事实不一定都说尽，但说出来的一定是事实，一定不要说谎，不要把自己吹嘘得天花乱坠，无所不能。说得太完美了，面试官也不会相信，轻则会认为你自我认知能力不够，重则会认为你职业操守有问题。坦然面对我们过往工作经历中的一些曲折，也是一种职业品质和潇洒。

7. 忌讳言谈举止非职业化

人在职场就要职业化。言谈举止不要太随意，不要用很世俗、江湖、随意的语言来介绍自己，应该用近乎书面的语言来表达。举止端庄即可，不要摇头晃脑、表情过于丰富，眼光尽量直视面试官。

二、自我介绍中的修饰性词语

在自我介绍时，可以多使用一些修饰性词语，使面试官更加深入地了解你，从而留下深刻印象。例如：

mature, dynamic and honest 思想成熟，精明能干，为人诚实

excellent ability of systematical management 有极强的系统管理能力

ability to work independently, mature and resourceful 能够独立工作、思想成熟、应变能力强

a person with ability plus flexibility should apply 需要有能力及适应力强的人

a stable personality and high sense of responsibility 个性稳重、具高度责任感

work well with a multi-cultural and diverse work force 能够和具有不同文化背景的工作人员配合好工作

bright, aggressive applicants 开朗、有进取心的应聘者

ambitious attitude essential 有雄心壮志

initiative, independent and good communication skill 积极主动、独立工作能力强，有良好的交际技能

willing to work under pressure with leadership quality 愿意在工作中承担压力，具备领导素质

willing to assume responsibilities 应聘者须勇于挑重担

mature, self-motivated and strong interpersonal skills 思想成熟、上进心强，有良好的人际交往能力

energetic, fashion-minded person 精力旺盛、思想新潮

with a pleasant mature attitude 开朗成熟

strong determination to succeed 有获得成功的坚定决心

strong leadership skills 有极强的领导艺术

ability to work well with others 有能力和别人配合好工作

highly-motivated and reliable person with excellent health and pleasant personality 上进心强又可靠者，并且身体健康、性格开朗

the ability to initiate and operate independently 有创业及独立经营的能力

strong leadership skill while possessing a great team spirit 高超的领导艺术和强烈的团队意识

be highly organized and efficient 工作很有条理，办事效率高

willing to learn and progress 肯学习进取

a positive and active mind 有积极、灵活的头脑

ability to deal with people at all levels effectively 善于同各种人员打交道

young, bright, energetic with strong career-ambition 年轻、聪明、精力充沛，并有很强的事业心

able to work under high pressure and time limitation 能够在高压力下和时间限制下进行工作

be elegant and with nice personality 举止优雅、个人性格好

with good managerial skills and organizational capabilities 有良好的管理艺术和组织能力

having good and extensive social connections 具有良好而广泛的社会关系

being active, creative and innovative is a plus 思想活跃、有首创和革新精神尤佳

with good analytical capability 有较强的分析能力

good presentation skills 有良好的表达能力

三、自我介绍中的新意

想要给评委留下深刻印象，不妨在平时也试试给自我介绍增添一些新意。

1. 以星座为话题做自我介绍

I'm an Aries. Arians are supposed to be courageous leaders but troublesome followers. Half true. I'm definitely a troublesome follower.

我是牧羊座的。牧羊座的人据说是很有胆识的领导人物，但同时也是很会惹麻烦的部属。说对了一半，我的确是个麻烦的部属。

I'm a Leo. Some good Leo traits are: broad-minded, loving, faithful. Bad traits are: bossy, patronizing. I'm a typical Leo. I'm faithful but patronizing.

我是狮子座。狮子座的优点是心胸宽阔、有爱心，以及忠诚；缺点则是专横、自以为是。我就是典型的狮子座，忠诚却又自负。

2. 以性格、职业为话题做自我介绍

I'm a person of principle. I do not compromise. Because I don't smoke, I do not wear a T-shirt with a Marlboro logo, even if somebody gives one to me free.

我是个有原则的人，绝对不会妥协。因为我不抽烟，所以我也不会穿印有万宝路字样的T恤，即使有人免费送给我。

Part VI   Supplementary Reading

A: Beijing Capital International Airport

Beijing Capital International Airport is located in the northeast of Beijing, capital of the People's Republic of China, and 25.35km from the Tiananmen Square, center of Beijing city. It is not only an aviation gateway of Beijing and a window for international communication, but also a radial center for China civil aviation network, featured in a large-scale international airport, with most important location, biggest scale, fullest facilities and busiest transportation in China.

Beijing Capital International Airport, under the administrative control of Civil Aviation Administration of China (CAAC), officially opened on March 2, 1958. With the development of civil aviation business and the increasing volume of passengers and cargo transportation, it was expanded in a large scale. The Passenger Terminal 1, covering an area of 60,000m^2, with auxiliary facilities, including parking apron and car parks, officially put into service on January 1, 1980. Terminal 1 was designed to serve 60 flights daily and 1,500 passengers at peak hours. The facility at flight areas of the expanded Beijing Capital International Airport meets the 4E standards required by International Civil Aviation Organization.

With the continuous growth of quantity of international airlines to Beijing and the density of international flights, the Terminal was enlarged again from October 1995 to November 1999. The Terminal 2, covering an area of 336,000m^2 and equipped with state-of-the-art facilities, officially went into operation on November 1, 1999. Terminal 2 is able to handle 26,500,000 passengers yearly and 9, 210 passengers at peak hours.

Due to the excellent geographic location and service facilities at Beijing Capital International Airport, 66 domestic and foreign airline companies are participating in the operational business, including 11 domestic companies and 55 foreign companies. More than 5,000 scheduled flights are available to 88 cities in China and 69 cities abroad.

B: Hong Kong International Airport

Hong Kong International Airport (IATA: HKG, ICAO: VHHH) is the main airport in Hong Kong. It is colloquially known as Chek Lap Kok Airport, because it was built on the island of Chek Lap Kok by land reclamation, and also to distinguish it from its predecessor, the closed Kai Tak Airport. The airport opened for commercial operations in 1998, replacing Kai Tak, and is an important regional trans-shipment center, passenger hub and gateway for destinations in Mainland China and the rest of Asia. Despite a relatively short history, Hong Kong International Airport has won seven Skytrax World Airport Awards in just ten years.

HKIA also operates one of the world's largest passenger terminal buildings and operates twenty-four hours a day. It is one of the world's busiest airports, especially in terms of international passengers, and also the second busiest airport in the world in terms of cargo movements. In 2008, HKIA handled 48.6 million passengers and 3.63 million tons of cargo. It is the primary hub for Cathay Pacific, Dragonair, Hong Kong Express Airways, Hong Kong Airlines, Air Hong Kong (cargo) and Asia Jet (private).

C: British Airways thinks it has got the answer for flavorless airline food: umami

Airline food can take a beating on its way to the plate. It's cooked many hours before a flight, then rapidly chilled, wrapped, trucked, stored and reheated. This often leaves it overcooked, dry and tough. In the air, passengers lose about 30% of their ability to taste as a result of dry cabin conditions and high-altitude pressure inside airplanes. So even food that might be appetizing on the ground tastes bland at 35,000 feet.

For years airlines have added salt to give the food a semblance of flavor and ladled on sauces to combat dryness. Competition among carriers has intensified in business class and first class, and airlines now spend as much as $50 a person serving signature dishes from celebrity chefs. But for many travelers, it often still tastes like, well, airline food.

People typically buy tickets based on routes, pricing and loyalty programs, of course. There's little expectation for good food in coach, where airlines still serve hot meals on long international flights. But on board in first class and business class, the first thing passengers often think about is food, airlines say. "You could certainly lose a customer," said Adrian Jaski, British Airways' manager oversees catering performance in London.

Enter umami, the savory taste found in tomatoes, Parmesan cheese, mushrooms, Worcestershire sauce and other foods. British Airways had previously worked with Heston Blumenthal, a famous London chef, known as a practitioner of scientifically engineered dishes and creator of delicacies like snail porridge.

On a British television series, he first tried cooking food from scratch onboard a flight; it was chaos. He then prepared elaborate cold plates that took too long for flight attendants to serve. He even tried getting passengers to spray saline up their noses to moisten the palate. British Airways decided that wouldn't fly.

Then Mr. Blumenthal hit on umami as a breakthrough ingredient for high-altitude food. Umami is an intense flavor first identified by the Japanese and dubbed the fifth type of taste the tongue can detect, along with bitter, salty, sour and sweet. Mr. Blumenthal tweaked a shepherd's pie recipe to include umami-rich seaweed, for example. "You can't load more salt but you can definitely up the umami," he said on his show.

After that, British Airways began working with the London-based Leatherhead Food Research on more quantitative study. Thirty professional food tasters conducted a series of experiments on the ground and in the air and found the sense of bitterness in food was heightened at altitude.

In addition to low humidity, they found that cabin lighting and temperature affect taste—cold temperatures and gray lighting have been shown to dull the experience of eating. Stress levels of travelers also affected taste.

And the researchers agreed with Mr. Blumenthal that umami didn't lose its punch at high altitude and could be added to recipes to bolster flavors. Even for items like steak—notoriously difficult to serve aboard planes without ending up tough and dry from double-cooking—a crust made of umami-rich ingredients bolsters flavor. "It's a salt substitute without the sodium," said Sinead Ferguson, BA's menu design manager.

Over the past year, British Airways has altered its recipes to load up on umami-rich foods. And it has pushed catering companies to overplay particular tastes in sauces so that tastes will come through for even the driest palate.

One example: The airline is serving a special tasting menu from the Langham, one of London's grand hotels, in the first-class cabin of its Airbus A380 super jumbo jets, and several recipes were reworked for high-altitude eating.

For a pork cheeks dish, "we had to pack more lime and lemon grass into the sauce," said Kevin Levett, executive chef for production at Gate Gourmet in London, which caters BA's flights.

Subtle wines don't cut it at 35,000 feet. The key at altitude is to minimize any bitterness in red wine tannins, since altitude makes them stand out more, and maximize fruit in white wine, because that gives it more taste in the sky, according to Keith Isaac, general manager of Castelnau Wine Agencies, the wine buyer for British Airways' business class service.

"Wine could be overly expressive and that is good in the air," said Mr. Isaac, who so far this year has tasted 850 wines for his airline client. "To me, above all, it's fruit. I spend all day on fruit."

Other airlines say they try to tailor food and wine for parched palates, but most haven't gone down the umami road. United, Delta, American and Singapore Airlines, a carrier heralded for its food, say they serve some foods containing umami, for example, but they don't make an effort to pump up use of it.

One reason: Many customers have a difficult time noticing any difference. Skytrax, a London-based consultancy that polls travelers world-wide about airline service, says it has seen "no visible difference" in customer feedback on British Airways food. Moore, a London technology executive and top-tier flier on British Airways, says that while food service has gone downhill on shorter flights, he thinks food on long trips across oceans has subtly improved. On a recent flight to New York, "the beef wasn't quite as destroyed as it used to be," he said, and the bread rolls were soft, warm and tasty. Business class food, he said, "tends to be quite good."

Others say it's still airline food. "My test of a restaurant is simply whether I was served a meal I'd want to go back for," said Howard Long, also a gold-level British Airways customer, "and I've never had a meal on an airline I wanted to go back for."

But British Airways is undeterred. Internal customer-satisfaction surveys score food higher, the airline says, and it is continuing what it calls its "Height Cuisine" effort.

Steam ovens have been installed in first class to supplement the convection ovens airlines typically use. The new ovens are a gentler way to heat bread and pastry without hardening them.

The airline challenged Twinings, its tea supplier, to develop a blend that would work better at altitude. Typically regular tea blends get brewed to taste either too strong or too bland, said Christopher Cole, BA's food and beverage and product change manager. Research took six months, testing with aircraft water and factoring in the lower boiling point of water aboard airplanes.

The airline settled earlier this year on a tea that's a mixture of Kenya, Assam and High Ceylon teas.

The next piece of this high-altitude puzzle? Coffee.

"We haven't yet come up with something that is noticeably different," he said. But one promising blend will be tested in-flight after Christmas. With coffee, bitterness really comes through in-flight.

"It's a difficult nut to crack," Mr. Cole said.

D: Operation strategy of Azul Airlines

Sometimes Azul Airlines appears to defy gravity. In just four short years, the Brazilian startup captured 10% of the world's fourth largest aviation market. A pending merger will give it in total 15% market share and revenues of $2.1 billion. Azul's CEO David Neeleman said the secret to success was thinking small. Short hubs to under-service cities in a continent-size country.

"So we have service between cities that didn't exist. We have service to cities that didn't have their airline service. We have 43 cities that nobody else flies to but us."

Neeleman, also the founder of American low-cost flyer JetBlue Airways, says the strategy for Azul was unique.

"83% of the flights in Brazil have 120 people or less on them. So we have a plan to hold 118 people."

They shunned traditional aircraft like 737s, opting instead for small Brazilian-made Embrears and ATR turbo-props that could land in airports the competition couldn't. They give pilots extra training in specialized flight simulators. The runway at Rio de Janeiro's airport, for example, is one of the shortest in the hemisphere. Without access to cover at the airports in Sao Paulo city, Azul established its main hub in the wealthy, agricultural heart-land of Sao Paulo state. We boarded a round-trip flight from Campinas to Rio to get a close-up look.

Their planes are small. They only have 118 seats. But each passenger has their own TVscreen, and of course the snacks are free. Azul's client base is growing quickly. "It's more practical for where I live, and the service at Azul has been fantastic," she says. "Before, we went by car or bus," he says,"it was six hours and with toss and gas, it's more expensive than flying." A slow in Brazil's economy dealt a blow to the country's airlines, especially dominant players Gol and Tam. Both reported net losses and slashed domestic routes. Azul has scaled back expectations, but it's still expanding.

"This year we are gonna be about 20% growth and next year I think we are looking at 10 to 15%." Once its merger with a regional carrier Trip is complete, Azul will service 100 Brazilian cities, more than Gol and Tam combined. No international flights on the radar yet, but Azul could be in good position to change its mind as the Campinas airport expands and the World Cup looms closer.

Unit 3
如何巧答面试难题——博得评委青睐

Chapter I Family Situation

Part I Introduction

如何在英语面试口语对话中占据上风？首先是不是要熟练面试口语呢，然后掌握一定的英语面试技巧。学会英语面试对话技巧不难，以下就是一些相关的面试对话技巧。关于面试官提出婚姻状况时，无非就是想知道你的稳定性，所以按照以下英语面试口语去回答，就能比较符合面试官的要求。

一、面试官提出的问题

面试之初，应聘者一般都会被问及一些关于家庭情况的问题。例如，When did you get married?（你是什么时候结婚的？）What's your marital status?（你的婚姻状况如何？）What does your husband do?（你的丈夫从事什么工作？）How long have you been married?（你结婚多长时间了？）Can you tell me if you will get married and have a baby in the near future?（你在近期会结婚生孩子吗？），等等。企业面试时询问家庭问题不是非要知道求职者家庭的情况，探究隐私，企业不喜欢探究个人隐私，而是要了解家庭背景对求职者的塑造和影响。企业希望听到的重点也在于家庭对求职者的积极影响。因此，应聘者一般只需做简单的回答即可，没有必要深入介绍自己的家庭生活。

二、回答这类问题的思路

（1）这些情况对于了解应聘者的性格、观念、心态等有一定的作用，这是招聘单位问该问题的主要原因。

（2）简单地罗列家庭成员。

（3）宜强调温馨和睦的家庭氛围。

（4）宜强调父母对自己教育的重视。

（5）宜强调各位家庭成员的良好状况。

（6）宜强调家庭成员对自己工作的支持。

（7）宜强调自己对家庭的责任感。

Part II Glossary

New Words	
downtown	*n.* 市中心区；三分线外
suburb	*n.* 郊外
neighborhood	*n.* 附近；街坊；接近
gorgeous	*adj.* 华丽的，灿烂的
redecorate	*vt.* 重新装饰
convenient	*adj.* 方便的；适当的
status	*n.* 地位；状态；情形
primary	*adj.* 主要的；初级的
elementary	*adj.* 基本的；初级的
bakery	*n.* 面包房
extend	*vt.* 延伸；扩大；推广
affair	*n.* 事情；事务；私事
postgraduate	*n.* 研究生，研究所学生
intention	*n.* 意图；目的；意向
environmental	*adj.* 环境的，周围的
engineer	*n.* 工程师
environmental	*adj.* 环境的，周围的
Useful Phrases	
pass away	去世
far from	离……距离较远

Part III Useful Expressions

Appearance

1. My dad is very tall.
   我爸爸很高。

2. My mom is very short.
   我妈妈很矮。

3. My dad wears glasses.
   我爸爸戴眼镜。

4. My older sister is very elegant.
   我姐姐很文雅。

5. My little sister is slim.
   我妹妹很瘦。

6. My elder brother is very handsome.
   我哥哥很帅。

7. My mom is very beautiful.
   我妈妈很漂亮。

8. My grandma has a very kind smile.
   我奶奶的笑容很慈祥。

9. My grandpa looks very healthy.
   我爷爷看起来很健康。

10. I look very cute.
    我看上去很可爱

Living Condition

1. I live downtown. (I live in the downtown area.)
   我住在市区。

2. I used to live in a small village near the ocean.
   我曾住在靠海的一个小村庄里。

3. I want to live in the suburbs.
   我想在郊区居住。

4. I live in a very beautiful area with great neighborhood.
   我住的小区特别漂亮，附近的街道也很漂亮。

5. My house has a gorgeous view of the ocean.
   我家可以看到很漂亮的海景。

6. There are three bedrooms in my house.
   我们家有三间卧室。

7. Our house is the most expensive one in my area.
   我们家的房子在我们小区是最贵的。

8. Our house needs to be redecorated.
   我们的房子需要重新装修。

9. Our house is in a very convenient area.
   我们的房子在一个很方便的小区。

10. It is very close to subway stations and bus stops.

离地铁站和公交车站很近。

11. It is not far from supermarkets and schools.
    离超市和学校不远。

12. We have a small, but efficient apartment with everything in it.
    我们的公寓很小，但是很实用，里面什么都有。

13. Our house is small, but comfortable.
    我们的房子很小，但很舒适。

14. We live in the outskirts of the city.
    我们住在市郊。

15. Our neighborhood is peaceful and quiet, but not boring.
    我们住的地方很和谐并且很安静，但是不无聊。

16. We live in a high-rise apartment downtown.
    我们住在市中心的一幢高层公寓里。

17. Our neighborhood is busy, but I love the activity.
    我们住的地方很热闹，但是我很喜欢这种活跃的气氛。

Family Status

1. What is your marital status?
   你的婚姻状况如何？

2. Could you please tell me something about your family?
   你能告诉我你的家庭情况吗？

3. I am not married, and I am a single.
   我还没有结婚，还是单身。

4. I usually get together with my family on weekends, because we are all busy on weekdays.
   我通常在周末与家人聚会，因为我们在工作日都很忙。

5. I have been married for 5 years and have a son.
   我结婚 5 年了，有一个儿子。

6. I am 26 years old.
   我今年 26 岁。

7. What kind of work does your father do?
   你的父亲做什么职业？

8. My mother passed away.
   我母亲已经去世了。

9. Do you have to support your family?
   你得养家吗？

10. Would you like to tell me your parents' career?
    你能告诉我你父母亲的职业吗？

11. There are five people in my family: my parents, elder sister, younger brother and myself.
    我家总共有 5 口人：我的父母、姐姐、弟弟和我自己。

12. I have been married, and I have a gentle wife and a cute son.
    我已经结婚了，有一个温柔的妻子和一个可爱的儿子。

13. My parents are both honest peasants.
    我父母都是老实的农民。

14. My elder brother is a driver.
    我的哥哥是一位司机。

15. My wife is an office worker.
    我的妻子是一名办公室职员。

16. I got married last year.
    我是去年结婚的。

17. My husband and I live apart now.
    我和我的丈夫现在分居两地。

18. I live with my parents.
    我和我的父母住在一起。

19. My wife and I don't want to have a kid now.
    我和我的妻子现在还不想要小孩。

20. My daughter is in primary school.
    我的女儿已经上小学了。

21. I have a big and happy family.
    我有一个快乐的大家庭。

22. There are three people in my family.
    我们家有三口人。

23. My father works in a bank.
    我爸爸在一家银行工作。

24. My father used to work for a trading company.
    我爸爸曾经为一家贸易公司工作。

25. My mother teaches in a high school.
    我妈妈在一所高中教书。

26. My mom loves teaching little kids.
    我妈妈特别喜欢教小孩儿。

27. I have an older sister.
    我有一个姐姐。

28. My older brother is going to get married in May.
    我哥哥准备五月结婚。

29. I have a twin brother.
    我有一个双胞胎兄弟。

30. My little brother is in the elementary school.
    我弟弟在念小学。

31. My cousin works for Air China.
    我表姐在中国国际航空公司工作。

32. My niece works for a toy company.
    我侄女儿在一家玩具公司工作。

33. My nephew works for a bakery ...
    我的侄子在一家面包房工作……

34. I am an only child.
    我是独生子。

35. My grandparents live with us, so we are an extended family.
    我的祖父母和我们住，因此我们有个大家庭。

36. My grandparents are retired.
    我的祖父母都已退休了。

37. There is no hurry to get married.
    不急于结婚。

38. My wife works for the government.
    我妻子是公务员。

39. We have been married for 20 years.
    我们结婚已经 20 年了。

40. My husband died five years ago.
    我的丈夫在 5 年前去世了。

41. I believe it's a personal question.
    我认为这是个私人问题。

42. She's a retired school teacher in Beijing.
    她是北京的一位退休教师。

43. I don't think I will have any baby within 2 years.
    我想 2 年之内我不会要小孩。

44. I have been married and live in Shanghai now.
    我已经结婚了，现在住在上海。

45. We planned to have a baby after buying our new apartment.
    我们打算买了新房后再生孩子。

46. We are going to get married when both of our careers stay stable/are stable.
    我们打算等两个人的事业都稳定下来再结婚。

47. Getting a baby is a big affair, we won't make the decision until we consider it thoroughly.
    生孩子是个大事，我们只有经过认真思考后才会做出决定。

48. Since my girlfriend is still studying as a postgraduate in Beijing University, we will not get married until she is graduates in two years later.
    因为我女朋友现在还在北京大学读研究生，所以我们要等到她毕业两年以后才能结婚。

49. I'm not going to get married soon, and even if I do, I am going to keep working for a long time. My career is the most important to me.
    我并不打算马上结婚，即使结了婚，我也打算继续长期工作。对我来说我的事业是最重要的。

Part IV Dialogues

Dialogue 1

A: Mr. Sun, would you mind if I ask you some questions, which may sound impolite?

B: Ah, never mind, please.

A: Can you tell me how old you are?

B: I am 25 years old.

A: Are you married?

B: No, I am still single.

A: Can you tell me something about your family?

B: Ok. There are four people in my family, my parents, my elder sister and I.

A：孙先生，我可以问你几个听起来可能不是很有礼貌的问题吗？

B：啊，没关系，请问吧。

A：你能告诉我你多大了吗？

B：我 25 岁了。

A：你结婚了吗？

B：没有，我还是单身。

A：那你能告诉我你家里的一些情况吗？

B：好的，我家四口人，我父母，我姐姐和我。

Dialogue 2

A: Where are you from?

B: I'm from Hunan Province.

A: Could you tell me something about your family?

B: There are five people in my family, my father, my mother, my two elder brothers and I. Both my parents are retired. One of my elder brothers is a software engineer and the other is an environmental engineer.

A: Your application form says that you have two elder brothers. How do you get along with them?

B: We get along very well. They live in Canada, now.

A: Are you married?

B: No, I am still single. But I have a boyfriend and I am going to marry him this year.

A: What kind of people do you usually make friends with?

B: Friendship is very important for me. I just hope that my friends are the same as I am. Meanwhile, I expect that my friends' hobbies are similar to mine.

A: Would you say you have a lot of friends, or just a few?

B: Not so many, but not really just a few, either, I suppose.

A：你来自哪里？

B：我来自湖南省。

A：能介绍一下你的家庭吗？

B：我家共有五口人，父亲，母亲，两个哥哥和我，双亲皆已退休，一个哥哥是软件工程师，另一个是环境工程师。

A：你的履历表说你有两个哥哥，你和他们相处得怎样？

B：我们相处得很好。他们现在居住在加拿大。

A：你结婚了吗？

B：没有，我仍然单身。但我有一个男朋友，今年我们打算结婚。

A：你常与什么样的人交朋友？

B：对我来说，友谊很重要，我希望我的朋友和我一样珍惜友谊，同时，我也希望他们和我兴趣相投。

A：你认为你有很多朋友，还是只有一些？

B：我想不很多，但也不是只有几个。

Dialogue 3

A: How big is your family?

B: There are only three people in my family, my parents and I.

A: What do your parents do?

B: My father is a factory director of a technology company and my mother is a housewife.

A: Do you have any cousins?

B: Yes, I have one sister who is a middle school student.

A: How do you get along with her?

B: We get along well. She is preparing for college entrance exams now, so she often asks me questions on how to study. We often go swimming and play tennis together.

A：你家里有几口人？

B：我家里只有 3 口人：父母亲和我。

A：你的父母是从事什么工作的？

B：我父亲是一家科技公司的厂长，而母亲是一位家庭主妇。

A：你有表兄妹吗？

B：我有一个妹妹，她在上中学。

A：你和她相处得怎么样？

B：我们相处得很好。她现在正准备考大学，所以，她经常问我一些怎样学习之类的问题。我们还经常一起去游泳和打网球。

Dialogue 4

A: Could you tell me something about your family?

B: OK. There are five people in my family, father, mother, elder brother, younger sister and I.

A: Are your brother and sister still in school?

B: My brother has got a job and my sister is still in college.

A: What does your father do?

B: My father is a middle school teacher.

A: What about your mother?

B: My mother is a housewife.

A: Are you married?

B: I am not married yet and I live alone now.

A: Do you need to support your family?

B: No, my father and brother are doing that.

A: Have you finished school?

B: Yes, I have already graduated.

A：能给我说说你的家庭情况吗？

B：好的。我家一共有 5 口人，父亲、母亲、哥哥、妹妹和我。

A：你的哥哥和妹妹还都在上学吗？

B：我的哥哥已经工作了，妹妹还在上大学。

A：你父亲是做什么工作的？

B：我父亲是个中学教师。

A：你母亲呢？

B：我的母亲是个家庭主妇。

A：你结婚了吗？

B：我还没有结婚，目前一个人住。

A：你需要负担家里的生活开支吗？

B：不需要，我父亲和哥哥会负担的。

A：你现在已经毕业了吗？

B：是的，我已经毕业了。

Part V Tips

　　面试开始时，面试官一般会问及应聘者的家庭情况，如家庭人口及其工作情况、家庭经济来源及收入多少、来本单位面试是自己决定还是父母、爱人意见，等等。面试官问这样的问题有两个目的：一是面试刚开始时应聘者都有些紧张、情绪不稳定，问一些应聘者最熟悉也易于回答的问题，可使其放松一下，消除紧张；另一个目的，是通过提这方面的问题了解你的家庭和你的关系怎样，从而探知你是怎样一个人，家庭环境好坏及对你的影响，负担重不重。如果说前者只是为了引发话题消除紧张，那么后者可能是面试官的用心所在。因为任何一个单位，都希望新来的工作人员自身条件较优越，没有家庭负担或负担很小，有利于你的发展，可以精力集中于工作。

因此，当面试官问你的家庭情况并不厌其烦地提很多问题时，你应当把情况如实地讲出来，如果你的家境很好，你在回答中一定要表明，并使对方相信你在家中比较超脱，可以精力集中地工作。即使家庭有困难也要实事求是地讲出来，但必须讲明你克服困难的决心和信心，以及克服困难的措施。这样就能解除用人单位对你的顾虑，从而放心地录用你。另外，回答此类问题时语言要简明扼要，只需三言两语，讲清楚即可，千万别唠唠叨叨、废话连篇。

Part VI Supplementary Reading

A: Secrect mission of Air Force One flight attendant

The 89th Airlift Wing at Andrews spent the past six months on an unprecedented recruiting drive to lure enlisted men and women to volunteer for the job and, to a lesser extent, to attract pilots. When Air Force One and other planes in the iconic blue and white color scheme were on stops at Air Force bases around the country, the wing invited service members to come and take a look. Frequent fliers Secretary of State Condoleezza Rice and Vice President Dick Cheney made video testimonials. Despite the prestige the duty confers, the wing was having trouble finding the quantity and quality of candidates needed, and the right mix of ages and ranks to keep the operation from being top-heavy, says Maj. Kurt Kremser, a pilot who runs personnel in the wing. But the Air Force says the effort—a large part of it simply making it known that such jobs exist—is paying off. The service found enough attendants to fill spots in the year ended in September and is well on its way to filling openings for this fiscal year. The Air Force attendants start at about the same pay around $40,000 a year as senior commercial attendants, but they can eventually earn considerably more. They also receive flight pay and per diems when traveling, and hazard pay for flights that go to places like Iraq and Afghanistan. For some, the goal is to be selected to fly exclusively on the two 747s that serve President Bush, although those duties don't bring extra pay. Tech. Sgt. Christina Sheridan, 32, earns it by flying blind, deep in the belly of a C-17 cargo plane. She staffs one of two "silver bullets", Airstream-type trailers fitted out with communications suites, a compartment for the VIP and his or her aides, and lavatories. The trailers nestle inside the giant planes so no one knows a VIP is on board. "Some places you wouldn't want a blue and white to go", she says cheerfully. "I spend a lot of time in Iraq, Bagram [Afghanistan] and Kabul. We do the same cooking but we serve on plastic instead of glass." Staff Sgt. Jon Jackson recalls a trip where the "distinguished visitor," or DV, had approved a menu choice of steak or chicken for the entree. But the DV suddenly got a taste for salmon. So the plane radioed ahead and on a fuel stop in Ireland, attendants made a quick trip to procure salmon for 50 people. Sgt. Jackson, working with a tiny sink and a cutting board in the rear galley, did his best to fillet and cook the fish himself. "Some things we can't do," says Tech. Sgt. Monique Townsend, who has spent seven of her 18 years in the service as an attendant. "You can't always get 50 pieces of mahi-mahi," she says. But "When are we going to eat?" are the first words out of their mouths. Food is No. 1. That was evident when Airman Fauci contacted the defense secretary's office to discuss meal preferences for the trip to College Station and back. Pulled-pork sandwiches won out over chicken fettuccini for lunch on the outbound leg. Buffalo chicken salad and steak fajita wraps, the options for the return flight, lost out to chicken Caesar salads.

B: What kind of right does the airline passenger have?

Your flight gets canceled and the airline says it doesn't have a seat for you for a full day. But you find another airline has a flight leaving in one hour. What to do?

Beg the airline to send your ticket to its competitor. Do it nicely, because there's no rule that says the airline has to help you.

How to regulate good service and fair dealings, if at all, has been a quandary for years. But stakes are higher now. The average airline load factor—the percentage of seats filled—rose to 82.8% last year, the highest for scheduled air services since 1945. With planes so full, airlines have limited reserve capacity to rebook customers after flights get canceled. Some passengers wait for days to get to destinations.

The Department of Transportation says over the last four years it has taken a more aggressive stance on passenger rights, pushing through regulations to curb long tarmac delays, increase compensation for ticketed passengers involuntarily bumped from flights and require airlines to always display the full price of airfares, including taxes and fees. Airlines let passengers either cancel or hold a reservation without penalty for 24 hours and reimburse baggage fees if bags are lost, because DOT requires them to.

Transportation Secretary Ray LaHood, who is stepping down after four years, said in an interview he became frustrated with airline service flying between Washington, D.C., and his home state of Illinois, and set out to force improvement. "When people are paying a pretty good amount of money to fly, they ought to be given the service they paid for and they ought to be treated with respect and treated like adults," he said.

The Republican supported passenger-rights legislation every year when he was a U.S. representative, but every attempt in Congress has failed. As DOT secretary, Mr. LaHood grew outraged at passengers stuck on planes for nine-plus hours in deplorable conditions, and pushed through hefty penalties for airlines that keep people on planes longer than three hours without a chance to deplane. The tarmac delay rule has dramatically curbed lengthy strandings.

Passengers have some other protections:

Airlines typically provide meals and hotels when travelers are stranded overnight because of an airline problem, though not because of weather or other exceptions.

When airlines lose bags, they're on the hook to pay out as much as $3,300 per passenger for domestic trips. (Carriers set the value of possessions lost, however.)

Fliers bumped from overbooked flights and stuck for hours are entitled to four times their ticket price, up to $1,300, on the spot in cash.

But beyond overbooking, baggage and tarmac delays, government and Congress have largely struggled to figure out rules and requirements. Last year Congress created a four-member committee to advise the DOT on what passenger protections were needed.

The panel, which included airline and airport officials, advocated some basic principles like knowing the cost of the entire trip before purchasing a ticket.

The only firm recommendation? That DOT require airports and airlines to provide "animal relief areas".

Passenger advocates say plenty more should be done. "Passengers have very few rights and many of the ones on paper are not really enforced," says Paul Hudson, executive director of the nonprofit Aviation Consumer Action Project, which advocates for airline passengers.

One of the biggest problems, Mr. Hudson says, is that Congress exempted airlines from state laws so consumers can only take disputes to federal court, not state court. That raises the cost and the legal threshold to sue an airline. "In every other industry you have consumer protection laws that are state and local," Mr. Hudson said. "Airlines argue they can't be regulated by patchwork state laws, but Wal-Mart is."

Airlines for America, the industry's lobbying group, says air travel is almost always crossing state lines and airlines can't be subjected to a particular state's rules. Carriers have improved service on their own and responded to passenger issues without legislation or regulation that could raise ticket prices, the group says.

"Other industries are not subjected to such irrational rules," A4A Chief Executive Nick Calio said in recent Senate testimony.

When the industry was regulated before 1978, a federal rule known as Rule 240 required airlines to send customers to competitors if they canceled flights. Without Rule 240, passengers often can't use their ticket on another airline that might have available seats.

Eight years ago, the European Union established what seemed like far-reaching consumer protections, requiring that airlines compensate passengers for long delays and cancellations. The intent was to force carriers to reduce delays and cancellations due to light bookings.

But the groundbreaking effort didn't go particularly well. Passenger protections proved confusing and, to a large extent, hollow. Airlines were given a broad exemption for "extraordinary circumstances" and often refused to pay passenger claims. Little has changed.

The European Commission's latest stabs at regulation takes a more pragmatic approach. If enacted, it would give European travelers firmer protections than what U.S. passengers receive.

Earlier this month, the commission proposed revisions that would strengthen some areas for consumers and gave airlines more latitude in others. If an airline can't re-route a passenger within 12 hours, it would have to book a customer on another airline or train. But airlines would have five hours before they'd have to pay compensation for delays, instead of three hours.

"Cancellations are always worse for the passenger than delay," says Frank Laurent, a policy officer for the European Commission in Brussels who helped draft the rules. "This proposal is much more realistic."

The EC plan has been criticized by consumer groups as a watering down of passenger protections and by airlines as an unnecessary burden in compensation and rerouting. Mr. Laurent says the criticism from both sides probably means the proposal found middle ground.

"What we tried to do with this proposal," he said, "is to find a balance."

C: She'll go far: baby girl born on plane is given a million air miles

A baby girl born on a flight halfway from Dubai to Manila has received a birthday present: a million air mile points.

The Philippine carrier Cebu Pacific said, the baby named Haven, was the first to be born on a Philippine arrlines plane.

Haven's mother went into labour on Sunday, four hours into the flight and five weeks before her due date. Cabin crew found two nurses who helped with the delivery.

The lead cabin crew member Mark Martin said two flight attendants were also trained as nurses.

"To baby Haven," he said. "You are God's miracle at 36,000ft and we're blessed to have been an instrument in your safe delivery. You will always be my most memorable passenger."

Lance Gokongwei, Cebu Pacific's chief executive, said that to celebrate the birth, Haven would receive one million GetGo points, part of the airline's air miles reward programme.

Flight crew welcome baby Haven to the world.

The flight was diverted to Hyderabad, India, the airline said, to ensure the mother and baby received medical assistance for the premature birth.

Another passenger on the flight said she did not mind the delay. "It only happens in movies, and we're lucky to witness this miracle," Missy Berberabe Umandal wrote in a Facebook post.

Chapter II   Education

Part I Introduction

一些航空公司在招聘人才时，就把经验和能力列为首要的条件，而学历并不是他们重点考察的内容。但是，这并不是说他们就不重视学历，因为所谓的能力是需要用学历来证明的，学历能为能力的施展提供"敲门砖"。这就是说，如果一个求职者没有良好的教育背景，就很难过面试这一关，甚至面试的机会都少之又少，更别提要叩开名企的大门了。因此，确切地讲，航空公司，尤其是一些知名的航空公司在招聘员工时，既注重求职者的学历，又注重求职者的能力、经验和综合素质，这几方面是缺一不可的。

当面试官提出"你的学历不太高"的质疑时，求职者可以这样回答："尽管要继续深造会困难重重，毕业生就业市场上的竞争也很激烈，但我觉得我学到了很多知识，特别是学会了对自己负责和与不同类型的人合作共事。我相信我学到的这些知识会为我今后的工作奠定一个良好的基础，我会加倍努力，继续深造。"

这位求职者回答得很好。首先，他让面试官了解到了他会充分地考虑别人的意见，而不会把自己的意志强加给别人。其次，在他的回答中存在一些消极的倾向，但他明确表示自己会处理好这些问题，会变消极为积极。最后，他的回答方式实际上是在肯定自己，虽然面试官提出的这个问题有些宽泛，但求职者结合自己的个人情况回答得很具体。

当面试官提出求职者某学科成绩不太好时，求职者最好不要直接回答"数学""体育"之类的具体课程，如果直接回答并且还说明了理由，不仅代表求职者对这个学科不感兴趣，面试官还可能会怀疑求职者将来也会对要完成的某些工作没有兴趣。这种情况下，求职者可以这样回答："我可能对个别科目不是特别感兴趣，但是正因为如此，我会花更多的时间去学习这门课程。通过学习，对原本不感兴趣的科目也开始有了兴趣，对于本来就有兴趣的科目我自然学习得更认真，所以我的各门功课都不错，很平衡。"

综上所述，教育背景是对一个人学习环境和学习能力的概述。求职者在回答提问时要注意投其所好，比如，面试官问你"What course do you like best?"，这时你最好回答和所应聘公司相关的科目，这会让他留下你很有潜力的印象。注意几个关键的词语：degree（学位）、subject（科目）、department（系）、Bachelor degree（学士学位）、major（主修）、minor（辅修）。

此外，教育背景中还需要包括的信息有：

（1）学校/院系/专业/学位（原则：①匹配；②重点突出；③简洁）

（2）成绩（GPA 的多种算法）

（3）课程（选课程的主要原则：所学课程与申请岗位对应；写明获得了很高分数的专业课程）

（4）其他亮点（个人成绩，取得的成就等）

Part II Glossary

New Words	
background	*n.* 背景；隐蔽的位置
attend	*vt.* 照料；招待；陪伴
primary	*n.* 原色；最主要者
rank	*n.* 排；等级；军衔
education	*n.* 教育；培养；教育学
average	*vi.* 平均为；呈中间色
position	*n.* 工作；姿态；站位
president	*n.* 总统；董事长；校长
charge	*n.* 费用；指示；掌管；指责
recreational	*adj.* 娱乐的，消遣的
contribute	*vi.* 贡献，出力；投稿

续表

New Words	
institute	*vt.* 开始（调查）；制定
scale	*vi.* 衡量；攀登；剥落
scholarship	*n.* 奖学金；学识，学问
Useful Phrases	
in charge of	管理；负责
according to	根据
so far	至今

Part III　Useful Expressions

School and Graduation Time

1. Would you tell me what educational background you have ?
   请告诉我你的教育背景好吗？
2. Which school or college did you attend ?
   你上过哪个专科学校或大学？
3. Which university did you graduate from ?
   你从哪个大学毕业？
4. What kind of schools have you attended ?
   你上过什么样的学校？
5. What degree have you received ?
   你得到过什么学位？
6. When and where did you receive your MBA degree ?
   你在什么时间，什么地点取得的工商管理硕士学位？
7. I received my MBA degree from Beijing University in 1994.
   我于 1994 年在北京大学获得的工商管理硕士学位。
8. I graduated from middle school in 1988.
   我是 1988 年从中学毕业的。
9. I am a graduate of × × college.
   我是 × × 大学毕业生。
10. I am a college graduate.
    我是大学毕业生。
11. I have a B.S. degree.
    我获得了理学士学位。

12. I graduated from primary school in 1986, and entered middle school in September of the same year. In July 1992, after graduating from high school, I entered × × university.

我 1986 年小学毕业，同年 9 月进入中学。1992 年 7 月高中毕业后进入 × × 大学。

Profession and Course

1. What's your major in university ?
   你在大学主修什么？

2. Why did you choose this major?
   你为什么选择这个专业？

3. What is your favourite course ?
   你最喜欢什么课程？

4. What are your major and minor subjects ?
   你的主修课和副课都是些什么？

5. What are your favourite and least favourite subjects ? Why ?
   你最喜欢和最不喜欢的科目都是什么？ 为什么？

School Grade

1. What is your class rank and how many credits did you get ?
   你的排名是多少？ 获得了多少学分？

2. Why are your grades so low ?
   为什么你的成绩不是很理想？

3. How were your scores at college ?
   你在大学时成绩如何？

4. How about your academic records at college ?
   你读大学时成绩如何？

5. Did you get a good record in English ?
   你的英语成绩好吗？

6. Which band did you pass in College English Test ?
   你通过了大学英语考试几级？

7. How is your score in English ?
   你的英语成绩是多少？

8. In what subject did you get the highest marks ?
   你哪科得分最高？

9. What records did you get at middle school ?
   你在中学成绩如何？

10. How do you think your education will help the company ?
    你认为你接受的教育将如何有助于在本公司的工作？

11. They were all above average.
    成绩都在平均分以上。

12. They are above average B.
    平均在 B 以上。

13. Yes, I obtained 92 marks in English.
    是的，我英语得了 92 分。

14. I passed Band Four in College English Test.
    我通过了大学英语四级考试。

15. It's 88 points.
    我获得 88 分。

16. I got excellent records: 96 points average.
    我成绩优秀，平均 96 分。

17. I am ranked the second of my class in terms of average marks.
    我的平均分数名列全班第二。

18. I have already learned a lot in the classroom and I hope to be able to make practical use of
    it in business in your company.
    我在课堂上学到了很多知识，我希望能够把这些知识运用到贵公司的实际业务中。

School Activity

1. Were you in a leading position when you were a college student ?
   你读大学时有没有担任过学生干部？

2. Did you get any honors or rewards at your university ?
   你读大学时有没有获得过什么荣誉或奖励？

3. Were you involved in any club activities at your university ?
   你在大学有没有参加过什么社团活动？

4. What extracurricular activities did you take part in at college ?
   你在大学参加过什么课外活动？

5. Yes, I was president of Student Union of our university.
   有，我曾担任过学校的学生会主席。

6. Yes, I served as the monitor for two years.
   有，我曾做过两年班长。

7. Yes, I was the class commissary in charge of studies.
   有，我曾担任班级学习委员。

8. Yes, I got the university scholarship in 2004-2005 academic year.
   有，我在 2004—2005 年度获得了校奖学金。

9. Yes, I won the first place in the English Oratorical Contest of our university in 2004.
   2004 年我获得了校英语演讲比赛第一名。

10. Yes, I was in the chess club for four years.
    我四年都参加了象棋俱乐部。

11. Yes, I was a violin player in the college orchestra.
    有，我曾担任大学管弦乐队的小提琴演奏员。

12. Yes, I was on the college basketball team.

    有，我曾是大学篮球队队员。

13. I usually swim in summer and run in winter.

    我通常夏天游泳，冬天跑步。

14. I keep running every morning.

    我每天早晨都坚持跑步。

15. I participated in a recitation training class in my junior year.

    我在三年级时曾参加过朗诵训练班。

16. I usually take part in recreational activities.

    我经常参加文娱活动。

Part IV　Dialogues

Dialogue 1

A: Would you tell me what educational background you have?

B: Yes, sir. I graduated from middle school in 1986, then I entered Shanghai Polytechnics. I graduated in 1992. I have a B. S. degree.

A: What department did you study in?

B: I was in Department of Physics.

A: How were your scores at college?

B: They were all excellent.

A: What is your major?

B: My major is Business Administration.

A: How have you been getting on with your studies so far?

B: I have been doing quite well at college. According to the academic records I've achieved so far, I am confident that I will get my Bachelor of Business Administration this coming July.

A: How do you think the education you have received will contribute to your work in this institution?

B: I have already learned a lot in the classroom and I hope to be able to make practical use of it in your company. My specialization at the university is just in line with the areas your institute deals with. I am sure I can apply what I have learned to the work in your institute.

A：你能给我介绍一下你的教育背景吗？

B：好的，先生。我于 1986 年中学毕业后进入上海科技专科学校学习，并于 1992 年毕业。我获得了理科学士学位。

A：你在哪个系学习？

B：我在物理系。

A：你在大学的成绩如何？

B：各科成绩都很优秀。

A：你是什么专业的？

B：我的专业是工商管理。

A：到目前为止，你在校的学习情况如何？

B：我在学校的学习状况良好。根据目前我的学习成绩，我敢确定今年 7 月我一定能获得工商管理学士学位。

A：你认为你接受的教育将如何有助于你在本机构的工作？

B：我在课堂上学了很多东西，我希望能把它实际运用到贵公司的商务活动中去。我在大学所学的专业正好与你们所研究的领域相一致。我相信我能够把我所学到的东西运用到你们研究所的工作之中。

Dialogue 2

A: May I help you?

B: Yes, I've come in apply for the position as × × × department.

A: I'm Smith, the manager of Human Resources Department. May I ask your name?

B: My name is Zhang Xue.

A: Would you tell me what education background you have?

B: I graduated from × × × College. My major was aviation service.

A: Do you have any experience in this field?

B: Yes, I have been working in × × × Airline Company for four years.

A: OK. Do you think you are proficient in both written and spoken English?

B: Yes.

A: OK. I will accept you for a three months-period of probation. Is this satisfactory?

B: Yes.

A：要我帮忙吗？

B：是的，我是来 × × × 部门应聘的。

A：我是史密斯，人力资源部经理。你叫什么名字？

B：我叫张雪。

A：你能告诉我你的教育背景吗？

B：我毕业于 × × × 学院，所学专业是空中乘务。

A：你在这方面有经验吗？

B：是的，我在 × × × 航空公司工作了四年。

A：好的。你认为你在英语说和写两方面都很熟练吗？

B：是的。

A：好的。我们将有三个月的试用期，你满意吗？

B：是的。

Dialogue 3

A: Which school are you attending?

B: I am attending × × × University.

A: When will you graduate from that university?

B: This coming July.

A: What degree will you receive?

B: I will receive a Bachelor's degree.

A: What is your major?

B: My major is ×××.

A: How have you been getting on with your studies so far?

B: I have been doing quite well at college.

A: How do you think the education you're received will contribute to your work in our company?

B: I have already learned a lot and I am sure I can apply what I have learned to the work in your company.

A：你在哪个学校上学？

B：我在 ××× 大学上学。

A：你什么时候毕业？

B：今年七月。

A：你能拿到什么学位？

B：学士学位。

A：你是什么专业的？

B：我的专业是 ×××。

A：到目前为止，你在校的学习情况如何？

B：我学得不错。

A：你认为你接受的教育将如何有助于你在我们公司的工作。

B：我在课堂上学了很多东西，我相信我能够把我所学到的东西运用到贵公司的实际工作中。

Dialogue 4

A: Which university did you graduate from?

B: I graduated from Hebei University.

A: What was your major at university?

B: My major is ×××.

A: Tell me about the courses of your major in university.

B: I take more than 50 courses in university, including ×××, ×××, ××× and so on.

A: How did you get on with your studies in university?

B: I did well in university. I was one of the top students in the class.

A: What subject did you minor in?

B: I didn't minor in any subject when I was in university, but I attended English and computer courses.

A：你是哪个学校毕业的？

B：我毕业于河北大学。

A：你大学时主修什么专业？

B：我的专业是×××。

A：说说你在大学时所学专业的课程。

B：大学期间我修了50多门课程，包括×××、×××、×××等。

A：你大学时成绩如何？

B：我成绩非常好，我是班里最优秀的学生之一。

A：你辅修过什么专业吗？

B：我在大学期间没有辅修过任何科目，但参加过英语和计算机培训课程。

Dialogue 5

A:　Have you received a degree?

B:　Yes. In 2009 I received my × × × degree from × × × University.

A:　How about your academic records at college?

B:　In fact my records were excellent. My overall GPA was 9 on a 10 scale, which was the highest in my class.

A:　That's very impressive. Which course did you like best?

B:　English. It was both interesting and useful, so I showed a great interest in it.

A:　Did you get any honors and awards at college?

B:　Yes. I was awarded a scholarship from the university every year. In 2010 I participated in the National Contest of Math's Models and I won the prize.

A：你获得学位了吗？

B：是的，2009年我在×××大学获得了×××学位。

A：你大学时学习成绩如何？

B：事实上我每门课都非常优秀，我的总平均成绩按10分制是9分，是班里最高的。

A：那可真不错哦。你最喜欢哪门课程？

B：英语。因为这门课既有趣又实用，我对它很感兴趣。

A：你大学时获得过荣誉和奖励吗？

B：获得过。每年我都获得学校奖学金，在2010年我参加了全国数学模型竞赛，并获得了奖项。

Part V　Tips

　　刚踏出校门的新人尚无实际工作经验，面试者也无从询问"工作"本身的专业性问题，但可通过你就读的学校、所选修的课程、在校表现以及参加的社团来判断你是否具备做好这份工作的潜力与能力，那么你该如何在面试过程中谈论自己的教育背景，又该如何用英语表达自己的教育背景呢？想必各位已经把关于教育背景的词汇背了许多，那么怎样才能把这些词组织成句子，让你的英语活起来呢？我们来看看 Peter 在面试中是怎么谈论他的教育背景的吧。

Snow: Would you tell me what educational background you have?

Peter: Yes. I graduated from middle school in 1986, then I entered Shanghai Polytechnics. I graduated in 1992 with a B.S. degree.

Snow: What department did you study in?

Peter: I was in Department of Physics.

Snow: How were your scores at college?

Peter: They were all excellent.

Snow: What course did you like best?

Peter: I was very interested in business management. And I think it's very useful for my present work.

Snow: How are you getting on with your studies?

Peter: I did very well in school.

Snow: Which subject do you like least?

Peter: I think it was Chinese history. Not because the subject was boring, but the large amount of materials that had to be memorized. It left no room to appreciate the wisdom of great people in the past.

Snow: When and where did you receive your MBA degree?

Peter: I received my MBA degree from Beijing University in 1998.

Snow: Were you in a leading position when you were a college student?

Peter: Yes, I was president of the student union of our university, and I joined the Communist party of China in my junior year.

Snow: Did you get any honors or rewards at your university?

Peter: Yes, I got the university scholarship in 1994-1995 academic year, received the second—class award in the Olympic Mathematics Competition of our province in 1993.

Snow: Great. Were you involved in any club activities at your university?

Peter: Yes, I was on the university basketball team.

Snow: What extracurricular activities did you usually take Part in at your university?

Peter: I persisted in jogging every morning. I sometimes played table tennis and sometimes played basketball.

Notes:

1. 对话中 Peter 回答了面试官提出的关于他教育情况的问题。educational background 是指"教育背景"。graduate from 是指"从某所学校毕业"。我们都知道"上大学"可以用 go to college 来表述，但 enter 这个词也可以表示"上"某所大学。如 Peter 在文中提到 ...then I entered Shanghai Polytechnics（我就读于上海工业大学），polytechnic college 是指"多科性工学院，工学院"。

2. Peter 说 I graduated in 1992 with a B.S. degree.（我 1992 年毕业并且获得了理工学士学

位。）B.S. degree 就是 Bachelor of Science 的开头大写字母缩写，在写简历的时候，一定要弄清楚自己学历的英文标准翻译。一般来说，bachelor 是学士学位，国内正规院校统招本科生毕业时所获得的学位，master 是硕士学位，等等。

3. What department did you study in?（你就读哪一个系？）I was in Department of Physics.（我读的是物理系。）这其实就相当于在问，What's your major?（你的专业是什么？）对于这样的问题可以回答："My major is Physics." 或者 "I major in Physics." 都可以。

4. 面试官一般还会问你在大学的学习成绩，How were your scores at college?（你的考试成绩怎么样？）可以回答 They were all excellent.（门门都是优秀。）或者概括地说 I'm doing well at school.（我在学校成绩很好。）

5. 考官还会询问你对学校里哪些科目比较感兴趣，因为这样会从侧面反映你的能力倾向。Which subject were you least interested in?（你对哪一科最不感兴趣？）Peter 说是中国历史，因为有太多资料要背，以至于没有任何时间去真正欣赏前人的智慧。

6. 关于获得过什么学位这个问题你可以如实回答，当然，如果你很了解你面试的公司，说一些投其所好的科目也无伤大雅。Peter 后来还获得了 MBA 学位，MBA 我想大家都比较熟悉了，就是 Master of Business Administration（工商管理硕士）的开头字母大写的缩写。receive a degree from，就是指 "从某所学校获得某种学位"。

7. 对话中 Peter 讲述了自己在大学里除了学习成绩之外其他方面的表现情况，这对考官来说也是一个值得参考的地方。a leading position，是指 "领导职位"，Were you in a leading position when you were a college student?（你在大学的时候担当过什么领导职位吗？）Peter 说他在大学里担任过学生会主席，并且还入了党，应该是表现很积极了。president of Student Union，是指 "学生会主席"，join the Communist Party of China，是指 "加入中国共产党"。

8. Did you get any honors or rewards at your university? 是问在大学里有没有获得过任何奖励或者获得过什么荣誉。Peter 回答说，I got the university scholarship in 1994-1995 academic year.（我获得了 1994—1995 学年的校奖学金），scholarship，是指 "奖学金"，那么 full scholarship，就是指 "全额奖学金"。academic year，是指 "学年"，一般包括两个学期，学期是 semester。

9. Peter 还被问 Were you involved in any club activities at your university?（在学校里参加过什么社团没有，）club activities 在这里指 "大学里的社团活动"，比如篮球队比赛，象棋比赛，等等。Peter 说参加过篮球队，I was on the college basketball team. 参加某个球队，用 on 这个介词。

10. take part in extracurricular activities，是指 "参加课外活动"。Peter 还每天早上坚持慢跑，persist in doing something，是指 "坚持做某事"。

Part VI　Supplementary Reading

A: My ideal job–stewardess

Everyone has ideals. What is the ideal? Ideals are the goals that people sets of their goals. The ideal is the lamp, the black night; the ideal is the sail, the other side that we sail for success. Because of the ideal life, life is rich and colorful. If you are a drop of water, do you have an inch of land? If you were a ray of sunlight, do you light a point of the dark? If you are a grain, do you feed a useful life? If you are a screw with the smallest screws, do you always stick to your life, if you want to tell us what you thought, do you in the day and night to promote the most beautiful ideal?

My dream is to be an air stewardess or stewardess for short. I originally did not intend this, but I have contributed to this ideal is because of a film called "emergency landing". The film is mainly about a plane in the process of flight encountered problems, the explosions is about to occur. The air hostess on the flight not only calmed the panic situation and made the passengers less nervous. When the plane landed, they first evacuated the passengers, and finally left. No one knows when the the plane will blow up, if you do not escape in time, it is likely to have life risk. But they were not afraid. See here, I was impressed by the attendant spirit of self-sacrifice, I decided to be a stewardess. Another thing strengthened my resolve. That summer, I went to Guangzhou by plane. On the plane, I see the flight attendants are one of the natural and graceful, elegant and I think when the stewardess can follow along with the aircraft to a lot of places, an increase of knowledge. They also can know a lot of people of different personalities, this is a good job.

My ideal is to be a flight attendant, I think to be a stewardess is a very glorious thing, there will be many people watching you with envy when you walk in the airport, there are a lot of people who want to say "Hello! How beautiful" with you.

Sometimes when I look at the blue sky, I see a plane flying through the sky, leaving a long cigarette. I always think, I must be a stewardess when I grow up. I can fly in the blue sky every day. Make friends with the blue sky. I know the difficulty of being a stewardess, the more is the degree of self-cultivation, to learn a foreign language, to communicate with people, talking with people to have patience, be confident and generous, to learn to calm, learn to smile and politeness, which is to achieve the standard.

In a very young time, a girl always had high hopes for her ideal, because the stewardess can not only travel around the world, but also wear beautiful uniforms. So I need to fight, but the pressure is certainly some. I should stress as the driving force, realize my most eager ideal.

I have had my dream, and he guided me forward like a dream. The ideal one but lost, the flower of youth will be zero, I will firmly grasp the ideals, and towards my ideal continuous efforts.

B: Five Kinds of Goods Most Worth Buying at the Airport Duty-free Shop

You've heard it before: Most things at the airport area total rip-off. Traveling necessities like food, refillable water bottles, books, socks and electronics should always be packed from home so you can avoidinflated airport prices.

The costs of goods typically surge at airports because of supply and demand. An airport eatery or shop is a traveler's only option for a last-minute purchase or meal, so if a traveler is in a bind, he or she will shell out the cash. In addition, airport rent space is very expensive for vendors, so retailers often hike the prices of their products to make a profit.

However, some items in duty-free shops (otherwise known as tax-free) are actually worth the buy. So if you're in a scramble for a few things before your flight, we compiled a list of the best steals.

1. Alcohol

In duty-free shops, alcohol is a great steal without tax, and can be anywhere from 25%-50% off compared to domestic prices. Plus, according to TSA, you can bring up to 3.4oz on the plane, and mini bottles of alcohol are usually about 1.7 oz, so you can easily throw your purchase into your carry-on!

2. Tobacco products

Just like alcohol, you can also find great deals on tobacco products including cigars and cigarettes pre-tax.

3. Hair and skincare products

Premium beauty products can be up to 50% at duty-free shops.

4. Makeup

Similar to hair and skin products, you can find top-notch makeup at airports with huge discounts.

5. Magazines

Although magazines are on the pricier side at airports, if you want some light reading for the plane, you can still grab a copy for a few bucks. It may cost a little more than you'd usually pay somewhere else, but the price difference isn't huge. And if it'll get you through the flight, this purchase is worth it.

C: Economist: Aviation Business is the Ghost of a Feast

Airlines stand to lose heavily should the euro collapse.

Meetings of airline bosses are rarely cheerful events, profits being tighter than leg room in economy. But this year's annual gathering of the International Air Transport Association (IATA) should have been different. For a start, the airlines' umbrella group picked the most promising market to host the pow-wow, which was held in Beijing. Not only is air travel booming within and from China, but the country's airlines also made half of all global profits last year.

But as IATA delegates assembled for their gala dinner on June 11th at the Great Hall of the People in Tiananmen Square, there was a ghost at the feast. The topic on most people's minds was not the dozens of airports to be opened this decade in China, nor the quarter of a trillion dollars the host country is spending to become an aviation and aerospace superpower. On the contrary, all eyes were focused on the spectre of financial chaos in Europe.

The euro zone's troubles have already pushed many European carriers into the red. IATA predicts that there is a "serious risk" of bankruptcies. Indeed, Malev and Spainair, two fair-sized European airlines, have already gone bust. Several big airline groups, notably Air France-KLM, are trying to make deep cuts. The global industry's after-tax profits are forecast to fall from $7.9 billion in 2011 to \$3 billion this year; that is just 0.5% of revenue (see chart). And if the euro collapses? "It would be worse than 9 / 11," says Willie Walsh, the boss of IAG, which owns British Airways and Iberia.

Things feel all the worse because 2012 might otherwise have been a good year. Oil prices have moderated of late. Global passenger traffic has risen by 6%, faster than the long-term trend. Freight contracted in 2011, but is reviving in many markets (though not Asia). Asset utilization is 79%, up from 74% in 2009. Planes are relatively full, especially in America.

That is to say, the industry faces three risks besides a European meltdown. First, an oil-supply shock-resulting from an Iranian crisis, say-would send fuel prices sharply up again and wipe out profits. Some airlines, including KLM, are investing in biofuels, but full commercialisation looks far away. Others use financial hedges, but these are pricey and can backfire if oil prices drop. Delta is even now finalising a deal to buy an oil refinery.

The second risk arises from the flood of new planes due to be delivered shortly. Production snags at both Airbus and Boeing have kept capacity tighter than planned. If everyone uses their new planes to expand capacity, rather than to replace clunkers, there could be a lot of empty seats.

The final threat pits ghost against host. The European Commission's inclusion of greenhouse gases from aviation in its emissions-trading scheme (ETS) is opposed by over 30 countries, of which China is the most defiant. If a compromise is not found, European countries must levy hefty fines on offenders and may seize aircraft-which could set off a trade war. On June 12th the China Air Transport Association, which represents Chinese carriers, said that China would retaliate with similar measures.

The Chinese government has forbidden its airlines from participating in the ETS. It has even threatened to cancel orders placed by its airlines with Airbus. No coincidence, then, that thisweek's banquet was paid for by the European aircraft maker. The Chinese appear unbowed.

Chapter III Character Personality

Part I Introduction

在面试中，面试官可能会要求你列出几个描述你个性的词。这个问题可能会有其他类似的问法，例如："哪五个词最能形容你？"当然这个数字可能是三，也可能是另一个数字。给你一个建议，就是至少准备十个词来描述你的个性，以防你需要它们。

面试官之所以问这样的问题是因为想多了解一点你的个性。你提供的答案可以揭示你是谁以及你如何融入工作环境。通过你的回答面试官也能洞察你的自我感觉，这是一个定位你的员工类型的很好的指标。

描述你自己的个性可能有点困难，尤其是要用几个浓缩的单词来描述的时候。如果没有答案立即出现在你脑海中的话，问问你的朋友或同事，他们会如何描述你。通常情况下，你选择的词语不会因不同的面试而发生戏剧性的变化，因为你面试的往往是同一类型的工作。

当你被面试官要求描述自己的个性时，把重点放在与工作相关的特征上。你目前有哪些特点是面试官希望看到的？不要在面试过程中去揣测面试官的心思，但在设计清单时，一定要记住工作描述和工作环境，仔细地选择你的语言。你选择用来描述自己个性的词语应该是积极的、自我肯定的。不要在这一点上列出你的缺点！这不是面试官想要听到的答案。

例如，你可以回答：我感觉最好的五个词是"灵活""坚定""乐观""谦逊""有抱负"。我是家里第一个上大学的人，在家庭的支持下，这些特质真的帮助我顺利完成了我的学业，而且我觉得我的这些个性会帮助我胜任这份工作。

每次面试中肯定会出现的可怕问题是"你最大的缺点是什么？"也许这是面试官淘汰应聘者的方式，他们想看看谁真正为这个不友善的问题做了准备。面试官谈你的缺点这个话题时，通常是想洞察一下你在碰到紧张不自在的难题时，能否从容不迫地解决。

在回答这类问题时要记住：人无完人，千万不要说自己没缺点；不要把那些明显的优点说成缺点；不要说出严重影响所应聘工作的缺点。举个例子，如果你是一个没有经验的应届大学生，面试官一看你的简历会觉得你的实践能力差，不了解社会，那么你最好回答：我很努力，学习成绩很好，但是社会经验比有工作经验的人少这是我的缺点，所以以后要往这方面努力，希望得到前辈的指教。

无论如何，你可以通过准备答案，并遵循下面的方法免去部分尴尬。

一、不要回避问题

请不要给出千篇一律的回答，比如："我最大的缺点是过于追求完美 / 工作太拼命。"也许这是真实回答，但不幸的是，它会给面试官错误信息，他们习惯了听这些通用回答，会以为你想回避这个问题。

二、要诚实

深入挖掘自己，找到真正的缺点。把它们写在纸上，看看哪些可以在面试的时候说。如果你说的是让你烦扰的缺点，听上去会更诚实。回想你在以前工作中遇到的困难，或是经理对你的有用批评，这样你能想起真正的缺点。

三、不要说会影响面试的缺点

虽然我们刚才提到你应该诚实，但也要记住别太诚实。你要避开那些会影响你得到工作的缺点。例如，申请人力资源的职位却说不善于与人相处，或者想做销售却说不擅协商。不是让你一定要编缺点，但是挑个不会影响面试的缺点会好一些。

四、要谈到你为克服缺点做的努力

要说你为克服缺点做的事。这是你向面试官证明的机会，让他们知道虽然你有缺点，但你会主动克服缺点，也有办法克服它们。在某种程度上，你为克服缺点做的努力会被视作优点。

Part II Glossary

New Words	
character	*n.* 性格；特点
personality	*n.* 人格，人品，个性
introverted	*adj.* 内向的，含蓄的
extroverted	*adj.* 外向性的，喜社交的
assume	*vt.* 承担；认为；装出；呈现
responsibility	*n.* 责任；职责；责任感
organized	*adj.* 有组织的，有条理的
persistent	*adj.* 持续的；坚持不懈的
flexible	*adj.* 灵活的；易弯曲的
optimistic	*adj.* 乐观的，乐观主义的
confident	*adj.* 确信的，深信的；有信心的
initiative	*n.* 主动性；主动精神
independent	*adj.* 独立的；自主的
energetic	*adj.* 精力充沛的，充满活力的
frugal	*adj.* 节省的，节俭的；朴素的
diligently	*adv.* 勤勉地，勤奋地
supervision	*n.* 监督；管理
distinguish	*vt.* 区分，辨别；识别
prioritize	*vt.* 划分优先顺序；优先处理
enthusiastic	*adj.* 热心的；热情的；热烈的
stubborn	*adj.* 顽固的；顽强的
indomitable	*adj.* 不屈不挠的；不服输的
fragile	*adj.* 脆的；易碎的
vulnerable	*adj.* 易受攻击的；易受伤害的
diligence	*n.* 勤奋，勤勉
affinity	*n.* 密切关系；吸引力

续表

Useful Phrases	
get along with	与……和睦相处
sense of responsibility	责任感
take care of	照顾
make a promise	允许；允诺

Part III　Useful Expressions

Stating Your Character and Personality

1. What kind of character do you think you have?
   你认为自己是什么性格的人？

2. What kind of personality do you think you have?
   你认为你自己具有什么样的个性？

3. What kind of person do you think you are?
   你认为你自己是个什么样的人？

4. Do you think you are introverted or extroverted?
   你内向还是外向？

5. Do you have any particular strengths or weaknesses?
   你有什么特别的优点和缺点吗？

6. How would you describe your own personality?
   你如何描述你自己的个性呢？

7. What are your weaknesses?
   你的缺点是什么？

8. What are your strengths?
   你的优点是什么？

9. What personality traits do you admire ?
   你欣赏哪种性格的人？

10. How would your friends describe you ?
    你的朋友们怎样形容你？

11. I'm introverted.
    我性格内向。

12. I'm extroverted.
    我性格外向。

13. I'm a good team player.
    我是一个富有团队精神的人。

14. I'm a faster learner.
    我学东西很快。

15. I'm an honest and reliable man.
    我是一个诚实可靠的人。

16. I'm willing to assume responsibilities.
    我勇于挑重担。

17. I'm an organized and fluent speaker.
    我说话流利、有条理。

18. I'm a hard-working, persistent person.
    我工作刻苦，性情执着。

19. I am highly organized and efficient.
    我工作有条理，办事效率高。

20. I have strong organizational skills.
    我的组织能力很强。

21. I am honest, flexible and easy-going.
    我诚实、不死板而且容易相处。

22. I am an optimistic and confident girl.
    我是个乐观自信的女生。

23. I am a dependable and hard worker.
    我是一个值得信赖并且工作刻苦的人。

24. I like taking on new challenges.
    我喜欢接受新的挑战。

25. I like communicating with different types of people.
    我喜欢与不同类型的人交流。

26. I like working with different types of people.
    我喜欢和不同类型的人一起工作。

27. I can work under high pressure and time limitation.
    我能在高压力下和时间限制下进行工作。

28. I can work under pressure and get along with my colleagues.
    我能在压力下工作，并能与同事和谐共处。

29. I am energetic, drive to success and initiative.
    我精力充沛，有成功和创造的动力。

30. I'm a person with a stable personality and high sense of responsibility.
    我个性稳重，具高度责任感。

31. I am initiative and independent with good communication skill.
    我积极主动，独立工作能力强，并且有良好的交际能力。

32. I am an energetic and fashion-minded person with a pleasant mature attitude.

我精力旺盛、思想新潮，而且开朗成熟。

33. One of my strengths is my friendliness and open-minded attitude.
    我的优点之一就是待人非常友好、开朗。

34. I am an optimistic and confident boy and I like the feeling of flying in the sky.
    我是一个乐观自信的男孩，我喜欢在天空飞翔的感觉。

35. Sometimes I lack patience in what I am doing. However, I'm very careful with my work.
    有时我做事情缺乏耐心。然而，我对我的工作非常小心。

36. Working hard and being frugal are both virtues. I strive to practice these two virtues in my life.
    努力工作和节俭是两种美德。我努力在生活中实践这两种美德。

37. I am a highly-motivated and reliable person with excellent health and pleasant personality.
    我上进心强、为人可靠，并且身体健康、性格开朗。

38. I have positive work attitude and I am willing and able to work diligently without supervision.
    我有积极的工作态度，愿意并且能够在没有监督的情况下勤奋地工作。

39. I am very tolerant of people and have been told that this is one of my strengths.
    我待人宽容，别人都说这是我的优点。

40. I have the competence to learn in new work settings and cope with new work situations.
    我有能力在新的工作环境学习并适应新的工作环境。

41. I am an honest, hardworking and responsible man who deeply cares for my family and friends.
    我是位诚实、工作努力，负责任的人，我对家庭和朋友都很关心。

42. I am a hard-working person and a fast learner. I am very eager to learn, and I get along fine with people.
    我是一个勤奋的人，学东西也很快。我非常渴望学习，和别人相处得很好。

43. I have sense of responsibility. Only if leaders give task to me, I will complete it in time. And if I promise to my friends, I will never break my promise.
    我有责任心，能够及时完成领导交代的任务，从不违背对朋友的承诺。

44. I am not very patient. That's obviously bad. But I am working on it every day, trying to control myself and be more tolerant to the others. It's not easy, but I definitely made good progress in recent years.
    我不是很有耐心，当然这很不好。但是我每天都在尽力改善，控制自己，并且容纳他人。这不是很简单，但是近年来我已经有了很大进步。

45. I trust people too much. It is nice to live with such feelings, but it caused me many troubles in the past. However, as I am getting older, I can distinguish friends from foes much better.
    我太过于相信他人，能够带着这样的信任来生活确实很好，但是这过去也给我带来了一些麻烦。随着我年纪渐长，我越来越能分清敌友了。

46. Time management is a problem for me. However, I've improved myself by learning from my former supervisors how to prioritize daily tasks and how to delegate duties to others if required.
    时间管理对我来说是个问题。然而，通过向我的前上司学习，我已经提高了我自己，学会了如何按照优先顺序安排日常工作，以及如何在需要的时候委派他人负责。

47. I believe collective strength will be stronger than personal strength. To some extent, unity can inspire people to make more efforts in work without boring. This is why we should cooperate with the people around me.

我相信集体的力量要比每个人单独的力量更强大，因为团结在某种程度上能激励人们更努力地工作，而且还能让人不觉得乏味，这就是人与人之间为什么要合作的原因。

48. I lack general work experience because I spent many years in advancing my education. However, my education has prepared me for the job–I learned some skills that couldn't be gained as extensively in any regular job.

我缺乏一般的工作经验，因为我花了许多年的时间来提高我的教育水平。然而，我所受的教育让我为我的工作做好了准备——我学会了一些在日常工作中无法获得的技能。

49. I am active and naturally kind-hearted. I like to take care of the people around me. When my friends need help, I will do my best to help them without considering gains and losses. And I have strong sense of responsibility without giving up easily. I also like to challenge consistently to make further progress.

我有着积极的人生观，生性善良，喜欢照顾身边的人，朋友需要帮助，只要我能做到都会不计得失地伸出援手。而且我责任心强，做事有始有终，不会轻易放弃，再加上喜欢不断接受挑战，所以我觉得我是个不断要求进步的人。

50. I am too focused on my career. I believe I should always be improving myself. My work life and personal life were out of balance, as I was too focused on my work lately. Nowadays, it is easy to dismiss the boundaries between work and home, so I need to find more time for the family and to develop other interests. Though I always put my all into everything I do, knowing how to balance things is an important quality that I must improve.

我太专注于我的事业了。我相信我应该一直在提高自己。因为我最近太专注于工作了，所以我的工作和生活失去了平衡。现在，我很容易忽视工作和家庭之间的界限，所以我需要为家庭找到更多的时间，发展其他的兴趣。尽管我总是把一切都投入到我所做的每一件事上，但知道如何平衡事物是我必须改进的一个重要的品质。

Part IV Dialogues

Dialogue 1

A: How would your friends or colleagues describe you?

B: They say that I am a friendly, sensitive, caring and determined person.

A: What personality do you admire?

B: I admire a person who is honest, flexible and easy-going.

A: Describe your personality.

B: I would say that I'm a good listener and I'm very reliable. I am an extrovert because

I am chatty and sociable. I feel energetic in crowds. I would also describe myself as a professional who can handle stressful situations and a heavy work load.

A: What is the most important thing for you to be happy?

B: Different people have different ideas. I think the most important thing for me is to have a good relationship with my family members and my friends. My family has always been very close to each other, and my friends and I spend a lot of time together. Without that I would be much less happy than I am.

A：你的朋友或同事怎么形容你?

B：他们说我是个友好、敏感、关心他人并且有决心的人。

A：你欣赏哪种性格的人?

B：我欣赏诚实、灵活而且容易相处的人。

A：描述一下你的个性吧。

B：我想说我善于倾听,而且我很可靠。我是一个外向的人,因为我很健谈,很好交际。我在人群中感到精力充沛。我也会把自己描述成一个能够处理压力和繁重工作的专业人士。

A：最能使你感到幸福的事情是什么?

B：可能因人而异。对我而言,最幸福的事情就是和家人、朋友拥有良好的关系。我的家人之间关系亲密无间,我也经常和朋友待在一起。如果没有了这些,我想我现在的幸福感会大打折扣。

Dialogue 2

A: From reviewing your resume, I can see that you performed excellently in school. What I want to know is why you think you're right for this job.

B: I am always interested in news coming from your industry, and I'm deeply impressed by your company's performance. I admire and agree with the employee developmental values that the company has adopted. I find that my personal goals and ideas fit perfectly with the company's goals and mission statement.

A: What kind of personality do you think you have?

B: Well, I approach things very enthusiastically, I think, and I don't like to leave things half-done. It makes me nervous. I can't concentrate on anything else until the first thing is finished.

A: What would you say about your weaknesses and strengths?

B: I'm afraid I'm a poor speaker, however I'm fully aware of this, so I'm learning how to speak in public. I suppose my strengths are I'm persistent and a fast-learner.

A: How do you get along with others?

B: I'm very cooperative and have good teamwork spirit.

A: How do you handle change?

B: There is nothing that will always keep the same in the world. In fact, all the things are changing with time passing by, including me. I need to learn the good things and change my own bad habits while growing up. This is so called the transformation of life.

A：从你的简历，我可以看出你在校时很优秀。我想知道为什么你认为你适合这份工作。

B：我一直关注你们行业的新闻。同时我也很喜欢贵公司培养员工的企业文化。我觉得我的个人发展目标、理念和贵公司的目标完全吻合。

A：你认为你有怎样的性格？

B：嗯，我做事非常热心，同时不喜欢半途而废。这会让我很紧张，我必须把前一件事情完成之后才能做别的。

A：你认为你的缺点和优点是什么？

B：我不太擅长说话，我已经意识到这点，因此正在学习如何在公众场合说话。我想我的优点是很执着，而且学东西很快。

A：你和别人如何相处？

B：我能与人合作，富有团队精神。

A：你是如何应对变化的？

B：世界无时无刻不在变化，没有什么东西是一成不变的，包括自己，人总要学着长大，吸取好的东西，改掉自己的坏习惯，这样才可以称作是人生的蜕变！

Dialogue 3

A: What kind of person do you think you are?

B: Well, I am always energetic and enthusiastic. That's my strongest personality.

A: What are your strengths?

B: As I have said, it's diligent and industrious. On the other hand, sometimes, it's too hard-working and I am under too much pressure to make things perfect.

A: What qualities would you expect of persons working as a team?

B: To work in a team, in my opinion, two characteristics are necessary for a person. That is, the person must be cooperative and aggressive.

A: What makes you angry?

B: Dishonesty. It's unacceptable.

A: What are your personal weaknesses?

B: I'm afraid I'm a poor speaker. I'm not comfortable talking with people whom I have just met for the first time. That is not very good for cabin service, so I have been studying public speaking.

A: Are you more of a leader or a follower?

B: I don't try to lead people. I'd rather cooperate with everybody, and get the job done by working together.

A：你认为你是什么样的人？

B：嗯，我觉得自己精力很充沛，做事很有热情。这是我最大的特点了。

A：那你认为自己的优点是什么呢？

B：正如我刚才说过的，我工作特别勤奋认真。但是，有时为了尽可能把事情办得完美些，我又会让自己背上太多的压力，工作太辛苦。

A：你期望和你在一个团队工作的成员具备什么样的品质？

B：依我之见，作为团队中的一员，合作精神和进取精神两者必不可少。

A：什么最容易让你生气？

B：不诚实。这是我不能接受的。

A：你性格上的弱点是什么？

B：我想我并不善谈，我不能和那些我第一次见面的人们自如地交谈。这对客舱服务工作不好，所以我一直在学习在公众面前谈话的技巧。

A：你是一个领导者还是追随者？

B：我不会尝试领导别人。我宁愿和每个人都是合作关系，大家一起把工作做好。

Dialogue 4

A: What kind of character do you think you have?

B: Generally speaking, I am an open-minded person.

A: What is your greatest strength?

B: My greatest strengths are my strong will and endurance to the things I like. Of course, they are not natural. I was a long-distance runner in the past. And while I was running, no matter how tired I was, I would tell myself that I cannot stop. If I stop, I will be a real loser. On the contrast, if I insist on running to finish the competition, even though I am the last runner to across the finish line, I will still feel proud of myself.

A: What is your greatest weakness?

B: My biggest drawback is that I am a little stubborn. I am always insisting on my own opinion. I will not consider other's advice until I found I ran against the wall. But because of my stubbornness, I become a person who have strong will and indomitable character.

A: What have you done to correct your weakness?

B: At present, I will consider the advice which is given by the people around me first and find the best way to solve the problem.

A：你认为你是什么性格的人？

B：总的来说，我是个思想开放的人。

A：你最大的优点是什么？

B：我最大的优点是坚强的意志力和超强的耐力。当然，这是后天训练出来的结果。我曾经是名长跑运动员，在跑步的过程中，无论自己有多累，我都告诉自己要坚持下去，不可以停下来。如果停下来就失败了，我将会是个十足的失败者。相反，如果我没有放弃，即使我是最后一个跑过终点线的人，我同样会为自己感到自豪。

A：你最大的缺点是什么？

B：我最大的缺点就是我有点固执，我总有我自己的想法，只有当我碰壁的时候我才会考虑别人给我的建议。但是正是因为我的这份固执、这份执着，才让我锻炼了我坚强的意志和不屈不挠的性格。

A：那你做了些什么来改正你的缺点呢？

B：我想现在我会在做每件事之前，好好斟酌身边的人给我的意见，找到解决问题的最好方法。

Dialogue 5

A: What would you say about your strengths and weaknesses?

B: One of my strengths is my friendliness and open-minded attitude and also, I think I have a warm personality. But sometimes, I find it is hard to tell others when I don't like what they are doing.

A: Can you work under pressure?

B: Yes, I can! When I was in college, I served as the vice minister of the sports department of the students' union. There are a lot of activities which are held by the department, so I have accustomed to working under strong pressure. There was one thing that gave me the deepest impression. That is the college sports meeting, which is one of the largest activities in my college. Basically, it is arranged by the sports department. It included many details, such as arranging the location of each class, arranging the order of admission to the opening ceremony, arranging the time of every kind of competition and so on. I believe I can.

A: Have you ever failed?

B: In fact, I was growing up accompanied by the failures. Failure shows me the path to success. Only after make mistakes, I can understand more deeply what is right. I have always thought that it was not good if one's life always goes well. An easy life can lead people to become fragile and vulnerable, so failure is one of the most important teachers in my life.

A: What is your biggest failure?

B: My biggest failure was that I was too confident to succeed. When I was in the middle school, all the students were preparing for the final exam. I also managed to reviewing all the courses. But I reviewed in my own way and ignored the importance which is given by my teachers, then I got a bad result in the exam. This bad result hit me greatly and made me know that I should regard other's experience as the sun which can take me to the brightness.

A: How do you handle failure?

B: At present, I have learned how to face failures. I will adjust my attitude well when facing failures. I should regard the failures as a further step to the success. And find the reasons for failures to make sure that I will not make the same mistake any more.

A：你认为你的优点和缺点是什么？

B：我优点之一就是待人非常友好、开朗，而且我认为我的个性很热情。但有时候，我发现很难告诉别人我不喜欢他们的所作所为。

A：你能在压力下工作吗？

B：是的，我可以。因为我在读大学期间，曾经担任过学生会体育部的副部长，学校举办的很多活动都是由体育部来组织的，所以已经习惯了在强压下工作。有一件事情给我留下了最深的印象，那是学校的运动会，这是我就读的大学最大型的活动之一，通常都是由体育部组织的，组织校运动会包括很多细节，例如要安排好每个班级的位置，运动会开幕式的入场顺序，各项比赛的时间安排，等等。我相信我可以。

A：你曾经失败过吗？

B：我觉得我是在失败的陪伴下长大的，是失败让我看清楚通往成功的那条路，只有犯过错才能更深刻地理解什么是对的。我一直认为人的一生如果太顺利的话，反而不是件好的事情。安逸的生活会让人变得脆弱、不堪一击，所以失败是我人生中最重要的老师之一。

A：你经历过最大的失败是什么？

B：太过自信结果导致自己慢慢变成了自负，觉得自己很聪明，结果聪明反被聪明误。记得上中学的时候，期末考试前大家都在复习中，我按照自己的方法进行复习，忽略了老师所讲的重点，考试成绩很不如意，这给了我重重的一击，它启示我听从有经验的人的指点会让自己少走很多弯路。

A：那你是如何应对失败的？

B：目前，我已经学会了如何面对失败。当自己失败时，要学会及时调整自己的心态，千万不能让自己灰心丧气，要把这次失败看成是又向成功迈进了一步，要及时找出失败的原因，总结经验，不要再犯同样的错误。

Dialogue 6

A:　what are your strengths and weaknesses?

B:　Well, I am very patient and this is the most important quality for a flight attendant. And I am a good team player. I enjoy working with others. Although I am a college student and lacking of experience may be my shortcoming, I am a good learner, and I believe my diligence can make up for my shortcomings.

A:　What would your friends say about you?

B:　My friends said I am reliable, because I will fulfill all the promises that I made. I will not make a promise if I cannot do that. My friends also think I am an easy-going person. Because I like to consider the problems from the other's point of view, I can make friends with different kinds of people.

A:　Are you satisfied with your performance at your college?

B:　Yes, I am satisfied with my performance. I managed to do the things that I should do and treated every people around me sincerely. I have done my best to help my classmates and have never done something regretful.

A:　Do you consider yourself a success?

B:　The meaning of success is broad. For me success is to fulfill the goal that I have set. I will separate my ultimate goal into many small goals, and realize these small goals one by one so that I can get my ultimate goal in the near future.

A: What do you think will be the biggest challenge of being a flight attendant?

B: The biggest challenge for being a flight attendant is that they need to be willing to serve for others and like to devote. A flight attendant must provide the best service for the passengers and improve the image of his or her company, so he or she can bring more benefits to the enterprise.

A: Do you have any natural talent or skill, something that comes easy to you?

B: My passion and affinity are natural. I do not need to pretend to be friendly. I think it is simple to communicate with others. If you treat the people around sincerely, there will be no indifference between us. I believe everyone can become friend.

A: 你的优点和缺点是什么？

B: 就像我之前说的，我很有耐心，而这是乘务员最重要的品质。我是一个很好的团队合作者。我喜欢和别人一起工作。虽然我是一个大学生，缺乏经验可能是我的缺点，但我善于学习，我相信我的勤奋可以弥补我的缺点。

A: 你的朋友是怎么谈论你的？

B: 我的朋友都说我是一个可以信赖的人。因为，我一旦答应别人的事情，就一定会做到。如果我做不到，我就不会轻易许诺。而且他们觉得我是一个比较随和的人，与不同类型的人都可以友好相处。在我与人相处时，我总是能站在别人的角度考虑问题。

A: 你对你在大学期间的表现满意吗？

B: 我对我的表现很满意，在我上大学期间，我尽心尽力做我应该做的事情，而且真心对待身边的每一个人，尽我最大的努力去帮助他们。我没有做过让自己觉得遗憾的事情。

A: 你觉得你自己成功吗？

B: 成功的含义很广泛，对我而言我觉得成功是想法设法去完成自己设定的目标，我把我的最终目标分解成许多小的目标，而我一个一个实现了这些小目标，就可以在不久的将来实现我的最终目标。

A: 你认为作为一名乘务员，最大的挑战是什么？

B: 作为一名乘务员最大的挑战是能否真正拥有愿意为他人服务，愿意奉献的精神。作为一名乘务员就要为乘客提供最上乘的服务，搞好公司形象，为公司带来更多的利益。

A: 你有没有什么天赋或技能？

B: 我的热情和亲和力是与生俱来的，我不需要故意装出一副很友善的样子。我觉得与人沟通是件很容易的事情，只要是真心对待别人，人与人之间将不会冷漠，我相信所有人都可以变成朋友。

Part V Tips

如果面试官让你用几个词来概括你自己，他通常是想看你对自己是否有一定的自我认知。其实这类似于介绍一下自己的优点。如：适应能力强，有责任心和做事有始终，结合具体例子向面试官解释，使他们觉得你具有发展潜力。

　　面试就像推销一样，因为你要赞美你的个性、才能和专业。雇主希望雇用能按时上班的员工，而且要能与同事和睦相处，还要能提供优越的客户服务。雇主也重视雇员按时完成工作的能力，创造性思考的能力和成为公司团队中积极的、有贡献的成员的能力。

　　如果你是一个认真对待工作并且表现始终在巅峰状态的人，那么这是你在面试中应该突出的个性特征。雇主寻找的是对自己的工作有激情，而不是简单地消磨时间来挣工资的员工。如果你对自己的工作感到自豪，并努力不断地提供最好的服务，那么就把这种个性特质作为面试重点。

　　雇主看重那些每次都能把工作做好的员工。如果你习惯仔细检查你的工作以避免出错，每天的工作都列出"待办事项"清单，那么在面试中你要突出这个事实。

　　准时上班、按时完成工作是雇主要求员工必须要做到的事情。如果你是一个守时、专注的人，习惯为每一项任务提前一段时间做好准备，那么在面试过程中一定要向你的潜在雇主强调这些做法。因为这种做法表明，你不太可能让乘客等待，不太可能让乘客没人招待。

　　善良、和蔼和专业是雇主所看重的重要个性特征。有幽默感、沉着冷静、性格开朗都说明你是一个很容易相处和共事的人。对于面试空姐、空少这种服务性的职位来说，和蔼的性格、沉稳的个性也能在潜在的雇主那里获得额外的加分。

　　"能谈谈你的优点和缺点吗？"

　　这个问题主要考察你对自身基本素质的正确认识以及能否全面、客观地评价自己。回答时应注意以下几点：

　　（1）尽管这是你的主观评价，受个人自信程度、价值取向等影响很大，也就是说你所描述的优、缺点与实际情况可能不符，但你的陈述在一定程度上会影响面试官对你能力的判断。例如，你谦虚地说自己语言表达能力尚需完善，那么尽管你在此前的面试中语言流畅、结构清晰、层次分明，且能够充分利用非言语符号，但面试官下结论时多多少少会受到你自己否定性结论的影响。

　　（2）回答此类问题的时候，最好的方法是诚实、中肯地回答问题，并提供一个真实的性格特征。许多面试者倾向于用一个"众所周知的答案"来回答他们的弱点或强项。面试官很容易注意到这些答案，因为他可能已经听过几百次了。作为一个"社会人"，你实际具有的优点是很多的，如：勤奋学习、集体观念强、善于分析问题、人际沟通能力较强，甚至连听母亲的话、对爱情忠贞也是优点。但面试时一定要突出重点，即：非常出色的特质和与面试职位相关的优点。若你反复强调的优点其实很一般，就会适得其反了。

　　（3）谈缺点也应从两点出发：一个是"避实就虚"，谈一谈无关紧要的小缺点，而不要过于坦白暴露自己能力结构中的重大缺陷。此外，还有一个"投机"的办法，就是谈自己的"安全缺点"，就是那些在某些场合是缺点，但在另外一些场合下又可能是优点的"缺点"，如你与那些对工作不负责任的人很难相处，经常由于苛求自己做事十全十美而导致工作的延误等。不过这种"安全缺点"由于易让经验丰富的考官认为你是"油嘴滑舌"，所以应慎用。如果面试官让你说明你有这个弱点的理由，请确保不要牵连或责怪任何人。弱点就像我们身体的任何器官，它的外表不取决于任何人，也不能归咎于任何人。

　　（4）谈论优点应注意表情、神态、语调等，宜"低调"处理。在回答你的缺点时可能存在困难，回答有关优点的问题就相对容易些。只是你应该记住，你不应该因为与面试官讨论自己的优点而忘乎所以。有时可表示自己"更上一层楼"的希望和努力；谈论自己的缺点不要停留于缺点本身，可将重点放在自己克服缺点的决心和行动上。不论是优点还是缺点，一定不要泛泛而谈，可以结合事例具体说明。

根据你提供的这些答案，面试官将决定是否会录用你为公司工作。因此，尽你所能正确地回答这些问题，在任何情况下都要避免虚构自己的弱点。

"你的座右铭是什么？"

座右铭能在一定程度上反映你的性格、观念、心态，这是面试官问这个问题的主要原因。要注意，不要说那些太长的座右铭和引起不好联想的座右铭；不要说那些太抽象的座右铭；座右铭最好能反映出自己某种优秀品质。如："只为成功找方法，不为失败找借口"。

"你最崇拜谁？"

最崇拜的人能在一定程度上反映你的性格、观念、心态，这是面试官问该问题的主要原因。不要说自己谁都不崇拜或者说崇拜自己；不要说崇拜一个虚幻的或是不知名的人，也不要说崇拜一个具有负面形象的人；所崇拜的人最好与自己所应聘的工作能"搭"上关系；最好说出自己所崇拜的人的哪些品质、哪些思想感染着自己、鼓舞着自己。

当面试中触及自己的弱点时，请记住"金无足赤、人无完人"，任何人都有其长处，也都存在某些弱点。应聘者的弱点在面试中也时常被触及。一般应聘者在主考官触及自己弱点后，就觉得有些难堪、表情很不自然，甚至心情久久不能平静，从而影响了自己在整个面试中的情绪。

主考官提问触及应聘者的弱点，一般有两种情况：一是从应聘者的简历或其他材料中了解到的弱点；二是提问中无意触及了应聘者的弱点。但不管是有意还是无意，主考官并不是抓住应聘者的弱点不放让您下不来台，而是借此来观察应聘者应付于己不利情况的能力，进而评价其个性素质。因此，当提问触及自己的弱点时，千万不要悲观丧气，更不能胡猜乱想。聪明的做法是首先敢于正视自己的不足，保持心平气和的情绪。回答问题时要发挥自己的优势，想办法克服自己的不足。例如，你平时寡言少语，特别是在众人面前不善于表达，而这样的弱点又不是一下子可以克服的。那么在回答问题时，就要注意抓住问题的核心，言语虽少但力求内涵丰富、答案准确，这样你仍能转变劣势，得到好评。

"你是团队的领导者还是团队的追随者？"

当你面试一份工作的时候，你可能会遇到很多常见的问题，这个是其中的问题之一。虽然这个问题的答案乍看起来似乎是非黑即白、非此即彼的，但最重要的事情是你是要明白，面试官问这个问题并不像这个问题的表面看上去这么简单。回答这个问题的好的答案不应该是一个或另一个。请记住，不管你面试的是哪种类型的工作，大多数职位都要求有效率的员工。除此之外，即使你面试的是初级职位，你仍然需要具备团队领导能力。如果你申请的是管理职位，情况就更是如此了。你不仅需要能够成为一个可靠有效的团队领导者，而且你还需要成为一个团队的参与者。

因此，当面试官问这个问题的时候，他们并不是简单地寻找一个答案来说明你是一个领导者还是一个追随者。相反，他们正在寻找证据，证明你能够在形势需要时扮演相应的角色。在回答这个问题时，你也应该考虑一下你面试的具体职位。想想那些可能与那份工作相关的职责类型。回想一下招聘启事，以及与工作相关的内容。

如果可能的话，给出一个你如何能成为团队合作者或领导者的例子。例如，你可能表明了你喜欢在团队中工作的想法，因为在团队中人们更容易分享想法、一起工作，并最终在团队工作时做出更好的决定。当然，与此同时，你应该主动跟进进度，这表明你也很容易独立工作。如果你意识到这个职位更需要一个人作为团队领导者，也是同样的道理。在这种情况下，你可能会说你能独自工作得很好，因为你是一个有进取心、有责任心、有条理的人，同时，你也不介意以团队形式共同工作，并且明白在某些情况下团队的工作方式才是最好的。

Part VI Supplementary Reading

A: The Safest Airlines by Travel + Leisure

Travel + Leisure, a monthly publication from American Express Publishing Corp, decided to find out which airlines are the safest of all by reviewing the latest global safety rankings from the Air Transport Rating Agency (ATRA) and the Jet Airliner Crash Data Evaluation Centre (JACDEC), and combines the two annual rankings with other critical factors to determine the top airline rankings.

No. 1　Lufthansa

Named after the medieval Hansa League, Germany's longtime national airline was founded in the 1920s and relaunched after World War II. Lufthansa has an enviable safety record since established, while growing to a fleet of nearly 300 aircraft that serve more than 200 destinations.

No. 2　British Airways

BA's safety record is especially commendable given how many different types of aircrafts the company has flown since its 1974 launch, from Vickers Vanguard turboprops to Concorde supersonic jets. The airline even offers a modified version of its flight safety awareness training to the public.

No. 3　Qantas (tie)

Raymond Babbitt (Dustin Hoffman) famously quipped in Rain Man that Qantas has never had an accident. That's almost true: the Australian carrier hasn't had a fatal crash since 1951.

No. 4　Southwest (tie)

Long a passenger favorite, Southwest has proven that a low-cost, no-frills airline can also excel when it comes to safety.

No. 5　Cathay Pacific

Often ranked among the best for passenger experience and in-flight service, Cathay Pacific can also boast about its outstanding safety record.

No. 6　KLM

Founded in 1919, Koninklijke Luchtvaart Maatschappij is the world's oldest continuously operating commercial carrier. Over the next few years, the Dutch carrier (now merged with Air France) will replace its entire fleet with brand-new aircraft, including the Boeing 787 Dreamliner.

No. 7　Emirates

The Dubai-based carrier has logged only two accidents in its 28 years of operation. Always at the cutting edge of in-flight luxury, Emirates is renowned for its onboard showers, mini spa, lounge bar, and private "suites" with fully reclining sleeper seats.

No. 8　United / Continental

One of the largest mergers in aviation history, Chicago-based United and Houston-based Continental came together in 2010 to form one of the world's largest airlines-more than 1,260 aircraft serving 370 destinations. While the two airlines have had to overcome some cultural differences, both share a reputation for safety.

No. 9　Delta

With 164 million passengers in 2012, Delta is the world's single largest airline. The Atlanta-based airline's safety record is even more impressive when you consider that Delta has more than 1.8 million flights each year.

No. 10　US Airways

One of the oldest American carriers, US Air traces its roots to 1939 and a small regional airline serving the Ohio River Valley. It has become a giant of aviation, with more than 600 planes serving 200 cities. In the past few years, new technology, employee incentives, and a system-wide customer service campaign have also improved the airline's reputation in areas like baggage handling.

B: About ICAO

The International Civil Aviation Organization (ICAO) is a UN specialized agency, established by States in 1944 to manage the administration and governance of the Convention on International Civil Aviation (Chicago Convention).

ICAO works with the Convention's 191 Member States and industry groups to reach consensus on international civil aviation Standards and Recommended Practices (SARPs) and policies in support of a safe, efficient, secure, economically sustainable and environmentally responsible civil aviation sector. These SARPs and policies are used by ICAO Member States to ensure that their local civil aviation operations and regulations conform to global norms, which in turn permits more than 100,000 daily flights in aviation's global network to operate safely and reliably in every region of the world.

In addition to its core work resolving consensus-driven international SARPs and policies among its Member States and industry, and among many other priorities and programs, ICAO also coordinates assistance and capacity building for States in support of numerous aviation development objectives; produces global plans to coordinate multilateral strategic progress for safety and air navigation; monitors and reports on numerous air transport sector performance metrics; and audits States' civil aviation oversight capabilities in the areas of safety and security.

C: Chicago Convention on International Civil Aviation

The Convention on International Civil Aviation, drafted in 1944 by 54 nations, was established to promote cooperation and "create and preserve friendship and understanding among the nations and people of the world."

Known more commonly today as the "Chicago Convention", this landmark agreement established the core principles permitting international transport by air, and led to the creation of the specialized agency which has overseen it ever since–the International Civil Aviation Organization (ICAO).

The Second World War was a powerful catalyst for the technical development of the airplane. A vast network of passenger and freight carriage was set up during this period, but there were many obstacles, both political and technical, to evolving these facilities and routes to their new civilian purposes.

Subsequent to several studies initiated by the United States, as well as various consultations it undertook with its Major Allies, the U.S. government extended an invitation to 55 States to attend an International Civil Aviation Conference in Chicago in 1944.

These delegates met at a very dark time in human history and travelled to Chicago at great personal risk. Many of the countries they represented were still occupied. In the end, 54 of the 55 States invited attended the Chicago Conference, and by its conclusion on 7 December, 1944, 52 of them had signed the new Convention on International Civil Aviation which had been realized.

Known then and today more commonly as the "Chicago Convention", this landmark agreement laid the foundation for the standards and procedures for peaceful global air navigation. It sets out as its prime objective the development of international civil aviation "...in a safe and orderly manner", and such that air transport services would be established "on the basis of equality of opportunity and operated soundly and economically."

The Chicago Convention also formalized the expectation that a specialized International Civil Aviation Organization (ICAO) would be established, in order to organize and support the intensive international co-operation which the fledgling global air transport network would require.

ICAO's core mandate, then as today, was to help States to achieve the highest possible degree of uniformity in civil aviation regulations, standards, procedures, and organization.

Because of the usual delays expected in ratifying the Convention, the Chicago Conference presciently signed an Interim Agreement which foresaw the creation of a Provisional ICAO (PICAO) to serve as a temporary advisory and coordinating body.

The PICAO consisted of an Interim Council and an Interim Assembly, and from June 1945 the Interim Council met continuously in Montreal, Canada, and consisted of representatives from 21 Member States. The first Interim Assembly of the PICAO, the precursor to ICAO's triennial Assemblies in the modern era, was also held in Montreal in June of 1946.

On 4 April, 1947, upon sufficient ratification to the Chicago Convention, the provisional aspects of the PICAO were no longer relevant and it officially became known as ICAO. The first official ICAO Assembly was held in Montreal in May of that year.

During this march to the modern air transport era, the Convention's Annexes have increased in number and evolved such that they now include more than 12,000 international standards and recommended practices (SARPs), all of which have been agreed by consensus by ICAO's now 192 Member States.

These SARPs, alongside the tremendous technological progress and contributions in the intervening decades on behalf of air transport operators and manufacturers, have enabled the realization of what can now be recognized as a critical driver of socio-economic development and one of humanity's greatest cooperative achievements–the modern international air transport network.

Chapter IV   Hobbies and Interestes

Part I   Introduction

通过个性和爱好的问答，面试官可以初步判断面试者的性格特点是否适合职位的需要。性格外向的人往往容易给人留下热情活泼、思维敏捷但不深沉的印象，这类性格的人在面试时说话的节奏要适当放慢，语言组织得当，要注意给人以博学多才、见多识广的良好形象。性格内向的人则容易给人留下深沉有余、反应迟缓的印象，在面试时，这类性格的人要力争积极回答，并就某一重大观点展开论述，以弥补自己性格上的不足。兴趣爱好有助于员工愉快地工作，而且能够促使员工更加热爱本职工作，从事的专业岗位与自己的兴趣爱好相吻合也更有利于员工在工作中做出成绩。

永远要记住：面试官的时间都是宝贵的，他不会问你没有目标指向性的问题，他一定想看出来什么！面试不是纯粹的聊天，面试官的每一个问题都有其用意。应聘者在谈论个人的兴趣爱好时，需要选择与岗位要求密切相关、能说明自己具备某种工作能力的兴趣爱好。

兴趣爱好能反映求职者的个性、喜好、品德、心态等，通过兴趣爱好可以考察求职者人格结构的完整性和生活的丰富性。如果你没有什么兴趣爱好，业余生活很单调，你的个性结构就可能有缺陷。相反一个业余生活丰富多彩的人，他从生活中得到的乐趣和成就感会更多，稳定性会更高，从而能对本职工作起到积极有效的支持作用，而且工作中产生的疲劳与压力也可以在兴趣爱好中得到调整和缓解。所以：

第一，不要说自己没有业余爱好。

第二，不要说庸俗的、令人感觉不好的爱好。比如我喜欢打网游，或者看电视。

第三，不要真当成闲聊天。爱好广泛说明你是一个热爱生活的人，但你是来面试的，不是来展示你的生活丰富多彩的。有取舍地陈述，爱好说一两个，两三个即可。取舍的标准是，与职位有匹配，比如，应聘程序员，可以说爱下象棋或围棋，说明你爱动脑子，善于分析，逻辑性强。大多面试官会认为在业余爱好上爱钻研的求职者对于本职工作也一定能钻研。

回答面试官这个问题，需要注意以下四点：

第一，回答真实可靠。

有人爱瞎动脑子，去"创造"爱好迎合面试官，结果往往一不小心就溜到陷阱里了，真的假不了，假的真不了。当你开始介绍自己的爱好时，就要想到面试官会就这个具体的爱好进行深度追问。你答不上来就是造假，谎言一旦被揭穿面试到此为止。

第二，避免太险或太闲。

爱好不要太危险，如爱好探险。公司不仅有经营上的风险，还要随时承担员工带来的各种风险。聘用一个"探险家"，一旦有了情况，哪怕是在非经营时间，公司都要去解决。不解决，岂不是连基本的人性都丢了；解决，公司就得乱上一段时日，里外损失惨重。

太险的爱好是一种极端，还有一种太闲的爱好。爱养宠物，比如，养鸟、养鱼、养花，面试官会直接给你贴上"毫无斗志"的标签，这不是年轻人应该有的爱好。

第三，给对方正面联想。

不要说自己的爱好仅限于工作之余就是在家听音乐，上网打游戏，这是标准的宅男，会令面试官产生应聘者性格孤僻、不合群的感觉。从小学就开始练习书法，直到现在还经常参加各种书法竞赛，面试官就会对你的毅力及对书法艺术的造诣肃然起敬。

另外，切记不要贬低别人的嗜好，你可以说你喜欢拳击，但你不能说男人练瑜伽就女性化，如果面试官正好喜欢瑜伽，那就不太好。

第四，爱好勿成嗜好。

凡事过犹不及，爱好也要有度。和面试官讲爱好的时候，记住讲到适度为宜，不能把爱好讲成嗜好。比如，做销售，你可以和面试官介绍你喜欢喝酒，讲讲中国的酒文化，但你不能说你每天不喝不行，每天从床上起来就惦记着喝酒，面试官直接就会认为你嗜酒如命。

如果一个人下班后就知道柴米油盐，那么他应该是个家务型的人，缺乏情趣和格调，也许会是难以沟通的人。过于重视业余生活的人，也会有太爱吃喝玩乐，不务正业的嫌疑。因此，在回答这类问题时，应该不温不火，既要显示自己的情调与修养，又要展现自己的事业心，并以此为原则说明实际情况。

Part II　Glossary

New Words	
personal	*adj.* 个人的，私人的
fan	*n.* 迷，粉丝
biography	*n.* 传记
poetry	*n.* 诗，诗歌
softball	*n.* 垒球（运动）
detective	*n.* 侦探
relaxing	*adj.* 令人轻松的
classical	*adj.* 古典的

New Words	
craft	*n.* 手艺；工艺
creative	*adj.* 创造性的，有创造力的
gym	*n.* 健身房
sociable	*adj.* 随和的，好交际的
physically	*adv.* 体格上，身体上
workout	*n.* 锻炼
refresh	*vt.* 使恢复，恢复精神
alert	*adj.* 警觉的，警惕的
statesman	*n.* 政治家
original	*n.* 原文；原件
capture	*vt.* 拍摄
passionate	*adj.* 热烈的；激昂的
sincerity	*n.* 真挚，诚心诚意
badminton	*n.* 羽毛球
approach	*vt.* 着手处理
enthusiastically	*adv.* 热心地，满腔热情地
subscribe	*vt.* 订阅
periodical	*n.* 期刊；杂志
enrich	*vt.* 使丰富，使富有
fiction	*n.* 小说
imagination	*n.* 想象，想象力
logic	*n.* 逻辑
Useful Phrases	
be fond of	喜爱，爱好
team spirit	团队精神
half-marathon	半程马拉松
concentrate on	专心于，把思想集中于
to some extent	某种程度上
narrow down	（使）缩小

Part III   Useful Expressions

Stating Your Interests and Hobbies

1. What are your hobbies?
   你的业余爱好是什么？

2. Do you have any special interests ?
   你有什么特别的兴趣爱好吗？

3. What are your personal interests?
   你的个人兴趣是什么？

4. What kind of hobbies do you have?
   你有什么爱好？

5. What do you do when you are not working?
   你业余时间都做些什么？

6. How do you spend your free time?
   你怎么打发你的空闲时间？

7. What kinds of sports do you like?
   你喜欢什么体育运动？

8. Are you interested in sports?
   你喜欢运动吗？

9. What kind of book are you interested in?
   你对哪一类的书感兴趣？

10. Now let's talk about your interests and hobbies.
    现在我们来谈谈你的兴趣爱好吧。

11. I am a music fan.
    我是个音乐迷。

12. I enjoy reading biography.
    我喜欢读名人传记。

13. I usually read or do some sports.
    我常常读书或做些运动。

14. I have an interest in travelling.
    我对旅游非常感兴趣。

15. I am fond of swimming.
    我喜欢游泳。

16. I enjoy walking in the sunshine.
    我喜欢在阳光下漫步。

17. I listen to English songs most of the time.
    我的大部分时间都听英文歌了。

18. I enjoy writing poetry and playing softball.
    我喜欢写诗，喜欢打垒球。

19. I love to go to all kinds of music concerts.
   我喜欢去各种音乐会。

20. My favorite books are those about detectives.
   我最喜欢读书的是侦探小说。

21. I enjoy sports, music, films and books.
   我喜欢体育运动、听音乐、看电影、读书。

22. I like playing tennis because it keeps me healthy.
   我喜欢打网球，因为它能使我保持健康。

23. I sometimes go to the concert with my family.
   我有时会跟我的家人一起去听音乐会。

24. I enjoy running every day, usually I do 10 kilometres.
   我喜欢每天都跑步，通常要跑 10 千米。

25. I often go mountain-climbing with my friends on Sundays.
   周末的时候我经常跟我的朋友去爬山。

26. I am interested in watching TV or other relaxing games.
   我对看电视和其他能令人放松的游戏感兴趣。

27. I'm an outgoing person, and like hanging out with friends.
   我是个外向的人，喜欢和朋友出去玩。

28. I like travelling very much and I enjoy working with people.
   我非常喜欢旅游，喜欢和人打交道。

29. My hobbies are cooking every day and dancing on weekends.
   我喜欢每天做饭，周末的时候去跳舞。

30. I can't imagine how my life would be if there is no music in my life.
   我不敢想象如果我的生命里没有音乐会怎么样。

31. My favorite hobbies are reading books and listening to classical music.
   我最喜欢的爱好是读书和听古典音乐。

32. I'm a football fan. But I don't play and just enjoy watching football matches.
   我是一个足球迷。但是我自己不踢足球，我只是喜欢看足球比赛。

33. I like arts and crafts. I'm a creative person, and like doing things with my hands.
   我喜欢艺术和手工艺品。我是一个有创造力的人，喜欢做手工。

34. I really enjoy going to the gym because it's sociable. I've met lots of new people.
   我很喜欢去健身房，因为它是个交际场所。我在那里认识了很多新朋友。

35. I enjoy being physically active, and spend a lot of time playing sports and team games.
   我喜欢锻炼身体，我在运动和团队游戏上花了很多时间。

36. I work out at a sports club three times a week. I have been doing the workout for the last 4 years.
   我每周在体育俱乐部运动 3 次。过去这 4 年来，我一直这样锻炼身体。

37. I like almost all sports, and I enjoy both playing and watching. I especially like table tennis and rock climbing.
   几乎所有的运动我都喜欢。我不仅喜欢做运动，而且喜欢看比赛。我特别喜欢打乒乓球和攀岩。

38. After lifting weights for about an hour, I swim for half an hour. It's also a great way to refresh myself after a day's work.

做完 1 小时的举重练习之后，游泳 30 分钟。这也是在工作一天之后，放松自己的好方法。

39. I like playing football. Football is a very exciting game because it keeps you alert and I also enjoy the team spirit of football.

我喜欢踢足球。足球是一项极刺激的运动，它会使你保持灵敏，我也喜欢足球运动中的团队精神。

40. I enjoy reading biographies, especially those of well-known politicians, scientists, and artists. I can learn a lot from their life experiences.

我喜欢读传记，尤其是那些著名政治家、科学家和艺术家的传记。我可以从他们的生活经历中学到很多。

41. I like the novels of Dickens very mach. I've read almost all of them in Chinese translation. I wish I could read them in the original.

我喜欢狄更斯的小说。我读过几乎所有的中文译本。我希望我能读原著。

42. Recently I began to read short stories in English. It is difficult for me. But I want to learn English, and I want to read books in English.

最近，我开始读英语短篇小说。这对我来说有一定难度。但是我想学英语，我想读英语书。

43. I like cycling, skate boarding and listening to music. I like cycling just because it's fun and it's good in a big city like Tianjin because you generally get somewhere faster than anyone else.

我喜欢骑自行车，滑板，听音乐。我喜欢骑自行车，因为它很有趣，而且在像天津这样的城市，骑自行车很方便，你通常能够比其他任何人都更快到达目的地。

44. I enjoy running and staying healthy. I actually finished a half-marath on last week. I am also a board member of a local charity group that organizes community service programs like feeding the homeless and cleaning up trash off the streets.

我喜欢跑步和保持健康。我上周完成了半程马拉松。我也是一个当地慈善组织的董事会成员，我们组织社区服务项目，比如为无家可归者提供食物，清理街道上的垃圾。

45. My favorite hobby is photography and I love capturing nature in my camera. I'm very passionate about traveling to places to explore nature. It's not only about having a creative eye, but to practice with sincerity to get the desired results.

我最喜欢的爱好是摄影，我喜欢用相机捕捉大自然。我非常热衷于在旅行中探索大自然。摄影不仅仅要有创造性的眼光，而是要真诚地去实践，以获得想要的结果。

Part IV　Dialogues

Dialogue 1

A: Do you have any hobbies? What is it or what are they?

B: I am interested in watching TV or other relaxing games.

A: How do you spend your spare time?

B: I usually read or do some sports.

A: What kind of books are you interested in?

B: My favorite books are those about detectives.

A: Well, those books are really good. I like them too. What kind of sports do you like?

B: I like almost all sports, and I enjoy both playing and watching. I especially like badminton and mountain climbing.

A：你有什么业余爱好吗？是什么爱好？

B：我喜欢看电视，还喜欢一些令人放松的游戏。

A：你怎么打发你的空闲时间？

B：我经常读书或者锻炼身体。

A：你喜欢读什么类型的书？

B：我最喜欢侦探推理类的。

A：哦，这种书确实不错，我也喜欢。你喜欢什么体育运动？

B：几乎所有的体育活动我都很喜欢，不管是亲身参与还是观看。我尤其喜欢打羽毛球和登山。

Dialogue 2

A: Do you have any special interests?

B: I enjoy being physically active, and spend a lot of time working out at a sports club.

A: Do you think you are introverted or extroverted?

B: In fact, I wouldn't call myself extroverted. Sometime I enjoy being by myself very much. But other times, I like sharing activities with others too, especially during these last few years.

A: What kind of sports do you like?

B: I like playing basketball. Basketball is a very exciting game because it keeps you alert and I also enjoy the team spirit of basketball.

A: What kind of personality do you think you have?

B: Well, I approach things very enthusiastically, I think, and I don't like to leave anything half-done. It makes me nervous, I can't concentrate on anything else until the first thing is finished.

A：你有什么特别的兴趣爱好吗？

B：我喜欢锻炼身体，花很多时间在体育俱乐部运动。

A：你认为自己是内向型的还是外向型的？

B：实际上，我不能算是很外向的。有时我喜欢自己一个人独处。但是有时候我也愿意和别人一起玩，尤其是前几年。

A：你喜欢什么体育运动？

B：我喜欢打篮球。篮球是一项极刺激的运动，它会使你保持灵敏，我也喜欢篮球运动中的团队精神。

A：你认为自己性格如何呢？

B：嗯，我可以很有激情地接受任何事情，同时不喜欢半途而废。这会让我很紧张，我必须把前一件事情完成之后才能做别的。

Dialogue 3

A: How do you spend your spare time?

B: I spend most of my spare time reading and I subscribe to various newspapers, magazines and periodicals.

A: What kind of sports do you like?

B: I like playing football, I like the feeling of cooperating with others.

A: What kind of books are you interested in?

B: My favorite books are those about detectives.

A: Well, those books are really good. I like them too.

A：你的业余时间怎么度过？

B：我大多数空余时间都在阅读，我还订购了很多报纸、杂志和期刊。

A：你喜欢什么样的运动？

B：我喜欢踢足球，我喜欢与别人合作的感觉。

A：你对哪一类的书感兴趣？

B：我最喜欢侦探类的书。

A：哦，这种书确实不错，我也喜欢。

Dialogue 4

A: Now let's talk about your interests and hobbies.

B: Well, I like reading, walking, swimming, hiking and playing basketball.

A: You have a colorful life.

B: Yes. These hobbies have indeed enriched my life.

A: How do you usually spend your time after work?

B: I prefer to read novels with a cup of tea.

A: What kind of books interests you most?

B: I am interested in science fiction.

A: You seem to be a man of imagination and logic.

B: To some extent, I regard books as my good companion.

A: If so, you can benefit a lot from them.

B: That's for sure.

A：现在我们来谈谈你的兴趣爱好吧。

B：好，我喜欢读书、散步、游泳、远足和打篮球。

A：你的生活倒是多姿多彩。

B：是的，这些爱好的确丰富了我的生活。

A：那么，下班后你通常都做些什么？

B：通常我喜欢泡一杯茶来看小说。

A：最吸引你的是什么类型的书呢？

B：我对科幻小说很感兴趣。

A：看来你是个富有想象，又有逻辑思维的人。

B：在某种程度上，我把书当作我的好朋友。

A：如果这样的话，你会受益多多。

B：的确如此。

Dialogue 5

A: How do you spend your leisure time?

B: I like playing games and having sports. They are my favorite hobbies.

A: So, what kind of sport do you like most?

B: Oh, it's hard to narrow it down to just one. I like all kinds of sports, basketball, swimming, lifting weights and so on. I work out at a sports club three times a week. After lifting weights for about an hour, I swim for half an hour. I have been doing the workout for the last 3 years. Maybe it is just the reason why I am so energetic.

A：你业余时间都做些什么？

B：我爱玩游戏和体育运动，这是我最大的爱好。

A：那么你最喜欢什么体育运动？

B：哦，那可实在太多了，我喜欢各类体育运动，打篮球、游泳、举重，等等。我每周在体育俱乐部运动 3 次。做完 1 小时的举重练习之后，游泳 30 分钟。过去这 3 年来，我一直这样锻炼身体。也许这是我精力如此充沛的原因吧。

Dialogue 6

A: What do you do in your free time?

B: Well, I am passionate about photography and I like capturing the beauty of nature. That is also why I love traveling to places and exploring nature.

A: Those are good skills but how can you apply them to this position?

B: Since I am comfortable working with a system, it will be easier to manage my responsibilities. My creativity can help unveil a new perspective to the company.

A：你业余时间做什么？

B：嗯，我热爱摄影，我喜欢捕捉大自然的美。这也是我喜欢去不同的地方旅游，探索大自然的原因。

A：这些都是很好的技能，但是你怎么能把它们应用到这个岗位上呢？

B：既然我喜欢在一个体系内工作，那么我就更容易管理自己的职责。我的创造力可以帮助公司揭开新的视角。

Part V　Tips

在准备面试的时候，你无疑会准备回答与你的职业有关的问题，比如，"你为什么想在这里工作"和"你为什么想离开你现在的工作"，但同时你也需要为介绍你自己准备好答案，这个介绍包括你在工作之外的爱好以及兴趣。

面试官之所以问这个问题是为了了解你的真实情况——这一点尤其重要，因为他们需要通过了解你的个性、技能、经历和爱好等方面来推断你是否适合这个岗位。

虽然这个问题是关于你个人的，你应该诚实，但是你也可以通过巧妙的回答让天平向你这端倾斜，特别是当你觉得你的回答还没有让面试官印象深刻的时候。

当你思考要向面试官提及哪些兴趣爱好的时候，绝对不能如此回答"我喜欢通宵狂欢""花钱玩在线扑克"。这样的回答不会给你的面试表现增添任何色彩，所以绝对要避免提及任何可能让人反感或可能影响你的工作表现的兴趣爱好，例如酗酒或赌博。

此外，要避免诸如"看电视""听音乐"或"保持健康"等很难让人留下深刻印象的爱好，这些并不意味着什么，也不会给你作为某职位候选人带来任何价值。

体育运动一直是一个很好的爱好——所以如果你参加了任何形式的运动或健身比赛，这样的兴趣爱好能很好地向你未来的雇主证明你的人际交往能力。

如果你经常进行团体的体育运动——例如每个周末参加五人制足球比赛或者每月进行基本投球技巧训练，那么一定要提到它，因为这表明你能很好地融入团队、进行团队合作，还能体现你注重成果、喜欢竞争——这些都是职场所需要的积极的特质！

同样，如果你真正定期去健身房健身，而不是说你想保持健康，一定要详细解释你每周去健身房三次、遵循严格的健身计划是为了提高你的力量和耐力，等等。这是一个更详细的回答，它能体现你的坚持、投入和自律，而不是单纯地为讨好面试官而编造出的讨喜的爱好。

但是如果你不喜欢运动或健身呢？去健身房、踢球并不是展示你职业技能的唯一选择。如果你在当地的动物救助中心参与某种社区组织或做志愿者，那你一定要提到这样的经历，因为它表明你喜欢帮助别人，而且你是一个自信、善于交际的人。

如果你在空闲时间没有参与任何社区组织或团队活动，也不要担心，你在家里所做的一切同样也能让面试官印象深刻！或许你喜欢阅读相关行业的文章以了解最新的相关资讯，或许你喜欢在网上观看在线的教学视频以提高你的相关技能，等等，这些都能表明你非常认真地对待你的职业发展。

虽然这些都是展示你是一个完美候选人的好方法，但重要的是要把它们和一些个人爱好混合在一起，这样面试官才能很好地了解你是谁。如果你喜欢和家人在一起散散步，或者做些新的食物，告诉面试官吧！只要它能为你的面试增添色彩，就值得一提。

最重要的是：不要撒谎。说真的，这是不值得的。你迟早会被发现，如果他们发现你从一开始就对他们撒谎，你的未来雇主不会给你任何机会的。

"你有什么兴趣爱好？"

如果面试官问你这个问题，绝不是单纯地对你的兴趣爱好感兴趣。醉翁之意不在酒，他们正试图收集更多有关你本人个性的信息。

所以，招聘官到底想听到什么？哪种爱好最能展现你的技能？下面这些方面可能是面试官问这类问题的真正用意所在。

1. 你是否全面发展

"我没有真正特别的业余爱好，我太忙了。"这种回答简直糟糕透顶，虽然你是在告诉面试官你是个工作狂，但这真的不是一件好事情。因为，你除了自己的工作外，不懂得也不会去花时间给自己充电加油。面试官也许更希望看到的是你有不同的兴趣爱好。但是爱好别列太多，因为这也可能暗示你比较优柔寡断，而且你不可能有充足的时间投入到每种爱好上。

2. 团队型 or 独立型

在申请一些独立工作特质更加明显的职位时，如果你提到的是阅读、绘画、写作或园艺这类偏孤独型的爱好，面试官可能更倾向于选择你。不过，现在面试官可能更感兴趣的是听到一些团队型活动爱好，比如团体运动项目或群体志愿者项目。

这是因为现在大部分工作都涉及某种程度的群体互动和支持，如果你真的不喜欢运动或者团队活动，那么也请你表明自己是个喜欢帮助别人、自信且善于交际的人。

3. 你是否具备较强领导力

尽管并非所有的工作都要求你具有管理才能，但这些类型的活动项目还表现了你有做出改变的欲望。

4. 你是否不断强化自己的技能

如果你有坚持多年的业余追求，并且尝试让自己变得更好，你可能会被视为有恒心和毅力。例如，艺术或音乐方面的才能就可能被视为你被录用的一个加分项，因为它们能改善你的沟通、写作以及研究技巧。另外，求职者业余时间参与一些知识培训活动，比如，学习在线课程，也会被认为是自律的表现。

5. 你是否有使命感和毅力

面试官希望看到求职者在业余活动中也能设定目标。目标设定对任何工作来说都至关重要，面试官希望看到你有使命感和完成目标的决心。在描述自己喜爱的项目时，回答也有技巧，那就是对细节的描述，因为细节能加深别人对你有这种爱好的认可度。

6. 你是否有激情而不过度亢奋

对业余爱好有激情是面试官很欣赏和看重的一点。因为这证明你能享受自己所做的事情，无论它是分内工作还是业余事务。但是请切记：阐述爱好时不要过度亢奋，否则听起来像你要把兴趣作为主业。

7. 冒险型 or 保守型

如果你享受滑翔、冲浪、跳伞等极限运动，就是给自己塑造了无所畏惧、自我驱动的形象。这对于需要野心和勇气的销售类职位很有好处。但对于需要高度关注细节、方法偏向保守的工作来说，有这种特质的人未必是合适人选。类似的问题在求职面试中经常会被问到。通常人们羞于谈论他们最喜欢的兴趣爱好，而且被问到这样的问题时似乎还很惊讶。尽管如此，对于面试官来说，最重要的任务就是评估面试者是否具备该工作所需的某些特定技能，所以当面试官询问你的兴趣爱好时，他只是想进一步深入了解你，因为你工作以外的生活更能反映出真实的你。

如果之前你还没有给面试官留下深刻印象，那么可能你谈论几个令人印象深刻的兴趣和爱好后，情况能向有利于你的方向发展。你在空闲时间做的事情可能会突出你有趣的一面。你不会想错过这个机会的。

兴趣爱好反映了一个人的性格，对于刚毕业的大学生来说，"兴趣爱好"更是在面试中起了不容忽视的作用。个人的兴趣爱好其实主要体现在业余活动上，对于刚走入社会的学生来说，业余活动主要就是课外活动。

课外活动包括社会活动和业余爱好。丰富多彩的课外活动表示你希望丰富自己的社会经验，发挥多方面的才能。通过你所参加的课外活动，可以看出你的交际能力、个人修养、成熟程度和健康状况。比如说你当学生会主席的经历能够表明你人缘好、善处人际关系、有领导才能等。

因此，如果你曾参加什么课外活动，就如实说出来。这些活动可以成为雇主了解你的有利条件。课外活动对于刚刚走出校门的朋友来说，是找工作时的一个相当重要的条件。因为大学生的简历在工作经验部分一般会相对单薄，所以面试官常会以关于"兴趣爱好"的问题为引子，然后再延伸开来追问应聘者在校期间的社团经历、社会经历等，最终考察应聘者是否具有培养潜力，从而决定是否聘用。那面试时该如何谈论自己的兴趣爱好呢？

兴趣爱好的选择要与所应聘的工作相关

面试不是纯粹的聊天，面试官的每一个问题都有其用意。应聘者在谈论个人的兴趣爱好时，需要选择与岗位要求密切相关、能说明自己具备某种工作能力的兴趣爱好。比如，当你去应聘某个论坛的编辑工作时，你可以介绍自己平时喜欢逛论坛，不过前提是你真的是某些论坛的用户，对它们有所了解，且能简单地说出该论坛的亮点或者不足，而如果你还有做论坛版主的经历，就会是一个很好的加分项。

没有兴趣爱好怎么办？

对于兴趣爱好广泛的应聘者，只要选择与企业文化、岗位要求相关的兴趣爱好来回答这个问题就可以了。但如果应聘者没有兴趣爱好，该如何回答这个问题呢？

其实，每个人都会有自己的兴趣爱好，只是某些兴趣爱好可能不适合在面试场合来说，或者是某些爱好在大众眼中有些消极，应聘者担心说出来会给面试官带去不好的印象，所以便说自己没兴趣爱好。但凡事都具有两面性，看似消极的兴趣爱好可能只是大众的看法，也许在具体岗位上它就有积极的一面。

在面试中切忌说自己没有兴趣爱好。因为这会让面试官产生各种对你不利的猜测，比如这个人是不是很孤僻，对生活、工作缺乏激情，这个人会不会很难相处、不能适应团队工作，等等。万一你真没有兴趣爱好，那也可以说一些平时经常做或者比较熟悉的事。不过，如果你想拿看书、听音乐这种大众化的兴趣爱好回答面试官，一定要事先想到面试官可能会有的后续追问，比如"你经常看什么书""你最喜欢哪一本书""你喜欢听什么样的音乐"，等等。

兴趣爱好比较偏，与面试官沟通时该注意什么？

如果你的兴趣爱好不像听音乐、打篮球那样为大众所熟知，且与应聘的工作相关性不大，那可在面试谈论时舍弃不说。当然，如果你独特的兴趣爱好确实与应聘的工作相关，那也不要掩藏，只是当你向面试官解释自己的兴趣爱好时，一定要用通俗简练的语言来进行概括，并说出这一兴趣爱好让你有哪些收获或者能锻炼你的哪些能力；另外，你要注意以谦虚平和的心态与面试官沟通，切勿咄咄逼人，也不要因为面试官不懂便在言语中表现出不耐烦或者轻蔑的态度。不然，即使你所说的兴趣爱好与应聘的工作有关，也会让你扣分。

面试是一个全面考察应聘者个人能力与岗位要求是否匹配的过程，无论你谈及自己的何种兴趣爱好，都是为了证明你有能力胜任应聘的岗位。面试不是闲来无事聊家常，也不是为了证明你比面试官懂得多，这一切都是为了展示你是这个岗位的最佳人选。

Part VI   Supplementary Reading

A: International Civil Aviation Day–7 December

International Civil Aviation Day was set in 1994 as part of ICAO's 50th anniversary activities. In 1996, pursuant to an ICAO initiative and with the assistance of the Canadian Government, the United Nations General Assembly officially recognized 7 December as International Civil Aviation Day in the UN system.

The purpose of International Civil Aviation Day is to help generate and reinforce worldwide awareness of the importance of international civil aviation to the social and economic development of States, and of the unique role of ICAO in helping States to cooperate and realize a truly global rapid transit network at the service of mankind.

As the UN and world nations have now adopted Agenda 2030, and embarked on a new era in global sustainable development, the importance of aviation as an engine of global connectivity has never been more relevant to the Chicago Convention's objectives to look to international flight as a fundamental enabler of global peace and prosperity.

International Civil Aviation Day Theme

Every five years, coinciding with ICAO anniversaries (2014 / 2019 / 2024 / 2029 / etc.), the ICAO Council establishes a special anniversary theme for International Civil Aviation Day. Between these anniversary years, Council representatives select a single theme for the full four-year intervening period.

For 2015-2018 inclusive the Council has selected the following theme:

"Working Together to Ensure No Country is Left Behind."

B: Cabin Crew First Aid

A very important role as cabin crew is administering first aid.

Hands-only CPR

It is imperative when you find a casualty that is not breathing normally to carry out a chest compression first.

Ask someone to call for an ambulance (if you are not on board an aircraft) whilst you commence CPR. If you are on an aircraft the airline will have an emergency procedure in place where other crew members will assist the first person on the scene giving CPR.

Ideally the patient needs to be flat on a hard surface before your commence CPR, e.g. on the floor or on a table.

Place the heel of your hand at the center of the person's chest, then place your other hand on top of your first hand and interlock your fingers.

Get close to the patient to the side or straddle if more comfortable and position yourself with your shoulders above your hands.

Using your body weight press straight down onto their chest, in an ideal world it should be 5-6cm (2.25 inches).

Always keep your hands on their chest and release the compression allowing the chest to return to its normal position.

Repeat these compressions at a fast rate of between 100 to 120 times per minute, until an ambulance arrives or until you become exhausted. If you can share this procedure with someone else this will help.

CPR with rescue breaths

If you are trained in CPR including rescue breaths, you should give chest compressions with rescue breaths. However, if you are not confident, then use hands—only CPR instead, as above.

After every 30 chest compressions, tilt the patients head back and pinch the nose to make a seal and blow steadily 2 breaths into the mouth checking that their chest rises.

Continue with 30 chest compressions and two rescue breaths until the patient shows signs of breathing naturally.

Children over one year old

The main difference with a child to an adult is chest compression's using one hand only and push down by 5cm (about 2 inches).

Infants under one year old

Gently open the child's airway by tilting the head back and lifting the chin. Remove any visible obstructions from the mouth and nose.

Place your mouth over BOTH the mouth and nose of the child and blow steadily into their mouth, checking that their chest rises. Give five initial rescue breaths.

Unlike an adult, place 2 fingers in the middle of the chest and push down by 4 cm (about 1-5 inches).

After 30 chest compressions at a rate of 100-120 per minute give 2 rescue breaths.

Then continue the cycle.

Remember, training cabin crew in first aid can be very extensive but is a life time skill—not just for the working environment.

C: Brief Introduction of The Boeing Company

The Boeing Company is an American multinational corporation that designs, manufactures, and sells airplanes, rotorcraft, rockets, and satellites worldwide. The company also provides leasing and product support services. Boeing is among the largest global aircraft manufacturers, the second-largest defense contractor (the arms industry) in the world based on 2013 revenue, and the largest exporter in the United States by dollar value. Boeing stock is a component of the Dow Jones Industrial Average.

The Boeing Company's corporate headquarters are located in Chicago and the company is led by President and CEO Dennis Muilenburg. Boeing is organized into five primary divisions: Boeing Commercial Airplanes (BCA); Boeing Defense, Space & Security (BDS); Engineering, Operations & Technology; Boeing Capital; and Boeing Shared Services Group. In 2015, Boeing recorded $96.11 billion in sales, ranked 27th on the Fortune magazine "Fortune 500" list (2015), ranked 90th on the "Fortune Global 500" list (2015), and ranked 27th on the "World's Most Admired Companies" list (2015).

History

In March, 1910, William E. Boeing bought Heath's shipyard in Seattle on the Duwamish River, which later became his first airplane factory. Boeing was incorporated in Seattle by William Boeing, on July 15, 1916, as "Pacific Aero Products Co.". The Boeing Company's corporate headquarters were located in Seattle until 2001.

Environment

Environmental record

In 2006, the UCLA (The University of California, Los Angeles) Center for Environmental Risk Reduction released a study showing that Boeing's Santa Susana Field Laboratory, in the Simi Hills of eastern Ventura County in Southern California, had been contaminated with toxic and radioactive waste. Clean up studies and lawsuits are in progress.

Jet biofuels

Main articles: Aviation biofuel and Algae fuel

The airline industry is responsible for about 11 percent of greenhouse gases emitted by the U.S. transportation sector. Aviation's share of the greenhouse gas emissions is poised to grow, as air travel increases and ground vehicles use more alternative fuels like ethanol and biodiesel. Boeing estimates that biofuels could reduce flight-related greenhouse-gas emissions by 60 to 80 percent. The solution blends algae fuels with existing jet fuel.

Electric propulsion

For NASA's N+3 future airliner program, Boeing has determined that hybrid electric engine technology is by far the best choice for its subsonic design. Hybrid electric propulsion has the potential to shorten take-off distance and reduce noise.

Political contributions, federal contracts, advocacy

In both 2008 and 2009, Boeing was second on the list of Top 100 US Federal Contractors, with contracts totaling $22 billion and $23 billion respectively.

Boeing has a corporate citizenship program centered on charitable contributions in five areas: education, health, human services, environment, the arts, culture, and civic engagement. In 2011, Boeing spent $147.3 million in these areas through charitable grants and business sponsorships. In February 2012, Boeing Global Corporate Citizenship partnered with the Insight Labs to develop a new model for foundations to more effectively lead the sector that they serve.

The company is a member of the U.S. Global Leadership Coalition, a Washington D.C.-based coalition of over 400 major companies and NGOs that advocates for a larger International Affairs Budget, which funds American diplomatic and development efforts abroad.

Divisions

The two largest divisions are Boeing Commercial Airplanes and Boeing Defense, Space & Security (BDS).

Chapter V　Occupational Planning

Part I　Introduction

伟大的事业不是自动产生的。就像你想要在人生中取得的任何成就一样，一项成功的事业需要时间、努力，最重要的是，需要做好计划。出于这个原因，以书面的形式总结你的雄心壮志，从而形成一个职业发展计划，在帮助你阐明你的职业目标和提高你的专注力方面是非常有用的。

职业发展计划旨在列出你的兴趣、爱好、价值观和各项技能，以帮助你思考以下问题：

你现在取得了什么成就，你期望取得何种成就；

你喜欢什么，不喜欢什么，对什么有激情，有何种技能、经验和个性，以及这些跟你选择的工作有多紧密；

你的短期职业目标和长期职业目标；

你可能仍然需要获得的技巧、资质和经验；

劳动力市场现状、你的工作具体职责所在，以及你可能需要研究的其他工作要求等。

对你的职业进行详细规划是帮助你获得梦想工作的第一步。通过设定明确的职业目标和规划，你需要采取的步骤来达到你想要的目标，你可以更容易地实现你为自己制定的目标。

把你的职业规划写出来（而不是仅仅是头脑里有一个抽象的想法），也会让你有一些东西可以回头做参考，而且你可以更容易地衡量你的进步。从你的清单上勾选出每个已经实现的职业目标是一个令人充满满足感的过程，事实上这是在了解你正在取得的进步。

记住，职业成功的道路不止一条，在你制定了职业发展计划后，你可能会意识到，从目前的形式来看，这不是你想要的路线——所以灵活性是关键。不要害怕调整你的计划，甚至可以基于你所学到的重新建立一个全新的职业目标。制定职业规划是你花费时间进行的有价值的投资之一。重要的是，当机会出现的时候，要准备好抓住机会，而不一定非得为它们做好充分准备。

思考未来，你希望五年或十年后到达什么样的各位置呢?

这是在面试中及其常见的一个问题。这是一个开放性的问题，答案不是简单的"是"或者"不是"，需要你进行详细描述。在回答这个问题时，需要注意的是，这个问题没有标准答案。你回答这个问题的方式完全取决于你独特的个性以及你未来工作和生活的目标。

还需要注意的是，你的回答可能会引导面试官让他认为你是这份工作的最佳人选。所以，如果他听到你计划在不久的将来返回学校进修或者你有兴趣有一天能够开办自己的公司，这样的回答会让面试官觉得你不打算在这个公司待很长时间。因此，他会觉得选你可能不是一个很好的注意，因为你可能计划很快离开公司，对你进行培训是浪费时间和金钱的事情。

你的回答不仅要让面试官确信你是这个职位的合适人选，而且还应该表明你对自己的职业成长感兴趣。你的最终反应应该表明你已经深思熟虑过这个问题。最后，你需要证明你自己的职业目标与你面试的公司是一致的。

好消息是，这是一个你可以在面试前很容易做好准备的问题，你可以仔细考虑你的短期和长期的职业目标。记住，这些目标以及你自己独特的技能和能力应该符合公司的目标，所以在面试前尽可能多地了解公司的情况是一个好主意。找出公司未来的愿景，这样你就可以准备好展示你未来的目标是同公司保持一致的。做这种类型的研究，花时间准备好这个问题的答案会在面试中很好地发挥作用。

Part II Glossary

New Words	
objective	*n.* 目标
ambition	*n.* 追求的目标；夙愿
contribute	*vt.& vi.* 贡献出；出力
project	*n.* 项目，工程；计划，规划
occupation	*n.* 职业，工作
establish	*vt.* 建立，创建
academic	*adj.* 学院的，大学的
advancement	*n.* 前进，进步；提升
exert	*vt.* 发挥；运用
conducive	*adj.* 有助于……的
purser	*n.* 乘务长
exceptional	*adj.* 优越的；杰出的
motivation	*n.* 动机；动力
professional	*adj.* 专业的；职业的；*n.* 专业人士
intern	*n.* 实习生；（尤指）实习医师
qualify	*vt.* （使）具有资格
outstanding	*adj.* 杰出的；显著的

续表

New Words	
devote	*vt.* 把……奉献（给）
loyal	*adj.* 忠诚的，忠心的
enterprise	*n.* 企（事）业单位；事业
internship	*n.* 实习岗位；实习期
insight	*n.* 洞察力，洞悉；直觉，眼光
reputation	*n.* 名声；信誉，声望
supervisory	*adj.* 监督的；管理的
recruit	*vt.* 招聘；雇用
anticipate	*vt.* 预感；预见；预料
capability	*n.* 才能，能力
stewardess	*n.* （飞机上的）女服务员，空中小姐
cooperate	*vi.* 合作，配合，协助
permanent	*adj.* 永久（性）的，永恒的，不变的
budget	*n.* 预算
commission	*n.* 佣金
envy	*vt.* 羡慕；忌妒
Useful Phrases	
apply for	申请
set a good example	树立好的榜样
come across	偶遇；偶然发现
in terms of	根据；就……而言
be satisfied with	对……感到满意
think over	仔细考虑

Part III Useful Expressions

Stating Your Career Planning

1. What is your career objective?
   你的事业目标是什么？

2. Why do you want to work here?

   为什么想要在这工作?

3. What's your five-year work plan?

   你的五年工作规划是什么?

4. Have you given thought to your career?

   你是否认真考虑过你的职业规划?

5. Do you have any ambition for the future?

   你对将来有什么抱负?

6. What can you contribute to the company?

   你对公司能做哪些贡献?

7. How would you describe the responsibilities of the position?

   你如何描述这个岗位的职责?

8. Where do you want to be 5 years from now in your career?

   5 年内你的事业想达到什么水平?

9. Could you project what you would like to be five years from now?

   你能设想一下 5 年后你会是什么样子吗?

10. What specific goals related to your occupation have you established for yourself for the next ten years?

    未来 10 年中，你给自己确定了哪些与你职业有关的具体目标?

11. I am looking for a more challenging opportunity.

    我想找一个更具挑战性的工作。

12. I'm very interested in your company's training program.

    我对贵公司的培训计划非常感兴趣。

13. With my strong academic background, I am capable and competent.

    凭借我良好的学术背景，我有能力胜任自己的工作。

14. I want to do a job that can offer me the opportunity for advancement.

    我想找一个能给我带来提升机会的工作。

15. Working in this company can give me the chance to exert all my strengths.

    在贵公司工作能发挥我最大的能力。

16. I feel I can make some positive contributions to your company in the future.

    我觉得我对贵公司能做些积极性的贡献。

17. In five years I want to be a valuable part of this company and help it to reach its goal.

    未来的 5 年里，我想成为贵公司里有价值的一员，并希望帮助公司实现目标。

18. Your company has a great future and is conducive to the further development of my abilities.

    贵公司前途光明，有助于我个人能力的发展。

19. My goal is to become a purser, and to help my team members to achieve exceptional results.

    我的目标是成为一名乘务长，并帮助我的团队成员取得优异的成绩。

20. Based on the job description I really believe that I can find new motivation and challenges in your company.

根据这个职位描述，我真的觉得自己能在你的公司找到新的动力与挑战。

21. I think the ideal job should make use of the professional experience I have obtained, and offer me opportunity for advancement.

我认为理想的工作应该能发挥我掌握的专业知识，而且能为我提供升职的机会。

22. My college training combined with my experience as an intern should qualify me for this particular job. I am sure I will be successful.

我在大学所受的训练，加上实习工作经验，应该使我适合做这份工作。我相信我会成功的。

23. I want to put my knowledge and experience to use in a challenging position. In order to achieve this goal, I just want to work step by step.

我想把我的知识和经验运用到一个具有挑战性的工作中，为了达到这个目标，我只想一步一步地踏实工作。

24. I feel my background and experience are a good fit for this position and I am very interested in it. What's more, your company is outstanding in this field.

我认为我的背景和经验非常适合这个工作，而且我会这个工作也非常感兴趣，况且贵公司又是这个领域的佼佼者。

25. I would like to devote all to this career till I cannot contribute anything to this job. I will manage to fulfill my duties without any complain.

我会为了这个职业奉献我所有的一切，直到我不能再为我的工作付出的那一天。我会尽心尽力做好我的分内事而不会有任何抱怨。

26. I will bring potential benefit for the company because of my current ability and good attitude to service. I believe I can bring a lot to the company.

就我目前的能力和我愿意为人服务的心态，我可以做一个优秀的服务人员在组织中发挥最大的潜力，给公司带来更高效和更多的收益。

27. In five years I want to be a valuable part of this company and help it to reach its goal. I also want to manage a challenging project that will benefit the company.

未来的 5 年里，我想成为贵公司里有价值的一员，并希望帮助公司实现目标。我还想管理一个富有挑战性的项目给公司带来效益。

28. You are a top company and I am convinced there would be no better place to work. You provide your employees with an open working environment based on team work.

贵公司是一家顶级公司，我确信没有比这更好的地方可以工作。贵公司在团队合作的基础上为员工提供了一个开放的工作环境。

29. If I really love the career I choose, I will be one of the most loyal employees in the enterprise. I will put all my energy into the work and devote my life to the company.

当我真正喜欢上我选择的这个职业的时候，我会是这个企业里最忠诚的员工之一。我会把我所有的精力投入到工作当中去，我会把我的一生奉献给这个企业。

30. During my internship I worked for a few days in each of the departments of a company. This gave me a great insight into management techniques and how a big organization works.

在实习期间，我在一家公司的每个部门都工作了几天。这让我对管理技巧和一个大的组织如何运作有了深刻的了解。

31. My last job was not challenging enough. I was not motivated to wake up to work anymore. I liked my colleagues and boss, but I simply can't keep myself motivated anymore.

我的上份工作不是很具有挑战性，我没有足够动力起床上班。我很喜欢我的同事和上司，但却没有干劲了。

32. I want to start a family and have a good job, the one where I will deliver an actual value. That's all I want. I believe that your company is a right place to start realizing my dreams.

我想要组建一个家庭，有一份能体现我的实际价值的好工作。这就是我想要的。我相信贵公司是实现我梦想的正确的地方。

33. I would like to have a managing role in five years' time. However, I understand that I need to learn a lot, and I believe that this position is a perfect starting point for my career dreams.

我想在 5 年内担任管理职务。然而，我知道我需要学习很多，我相信这个职位是我职业梦想的一个完美起点。

34. Your company is known as a company that rewards employees who deliver good results. Its good reputation and successful strategies and values make everyone want to work for such a company.

我知道贵公司以奖励有优秀工作成果的员工而著称。良好的名誉，成功的战略和价值观，使得每个人都希望自己能够为这样的公司工作。

35. Although my initial focus would be to work to my full potential in the job I'm applying for, I would like very much to move into a supervisory or management role in 3-5 years or less. I enjoy supporting my team members, and strive to set a good example for others.

尽管我的首要目标是在我申请的岗位上全力以赴，但是我仍然很想在 3～5 年内，甚至更短的时间内上升到主管或者管理级别的职位。我很愿意支持团队成员，并想为别人树立一个好的榜样。

36. I fulfill all the job requirements. However, I am sure some other applicants do fulfill it too. But I am a nice guy and always try to create a good atmosphere on the workplace. This helps, especially nowadays, when people are stressed and negative about everything.

我满足职位需求的所有条件。虽然我相信还有其他的求职者也能满足条件，但我为人和善，总能在工作场合创造良好的氛围。这很重要，尤其是在现在更是如此，因为人们总是压力缠身，对一切充满负面情绪。

37. I love this career, I would like to serve for others. If one not wants to do so, he or she will not become a good severer. There will be no passengers that will hate the people who are sincere to them. Our responsibility is to provide the best service to make passengers satisfied.

我爱这个职业，我愿意为别人服务，而且是真心想要这样做的，如果一个人不具备这样的心态是当不好服务人员的，没有任何一个乘客会喜欢那个不是真心实意想要为自己服务的人，我们的工作和责任就是呈现我们最上乘的服务，得到乘客的认可，让他们满意。

38. Everything starts in a low place. Firstly, I should fully understand the career of flight attendants. Only after that I can become a qualified manager of flight attendants. I believe I

can recruit the best staff and inspire their potential ability to bring the most benefits to our enterprise.

一切还要从头做起，首先，我应该充分了解空姐这个职业。只有这样，我才能成为一名合格的人力资源主管，凭借我的能力为企业招聘到更适合的人才，挖掘他们的潜力，进行最好、最理想的人力资源优化配置，为企业带来更多的利益。

39. I have great customer service skills that can be demonstrated by my ability to meet and exceed customer expectations. I can recognize the prime importance of the customer and even anticipate future customer needs. I will take responsibility for developing long-term relationships with customers and forge partnerships that contribute to future growth opportunities for both customer and my own organization.

我有很好的客户服务技能，这点从我可以满足和超越客户期望来证明。我能意识到顾客认为是头等重要的事情，甚至可以预见到未来顾客的需求。我将负责发展与客户的长期关系，与他们建立伙伴关系，为客户和我自己的组织提供未来的成长机会。

40. I believe that you have come across many others who are equipped for the job in terms of capabilities and abilities; however, going through my past experience and work performance you will find out that I am one of the more dedicated individuals who take their professional lives as seriously as they take their personal lives. Therefore, I am sure that with my dedication and capabilities, I am one of the best options that are available for the said job.

我相信你已经遇到了许多具备从事这项工作能力的人；然而，查看我过去的工作经验和表现，你会发现，我是一个更有奉献精神的人，我对待职业生活和个人生活一样认真。因此，我相信凭借我的奉献精神和敬业精神，我是适合这份工作的最佳人选。

Part IV　Dialogues

Dialogue 1

A: Why do you want to be a flight attendant? What is the best part of being a flight attendant?

B: Stewardess is one of my favorite jobs. This job can take me to different parts of the world to experience the local culture, to see new things that I have never known, to meet different kinds of people in different careers and so on. As we known, the life is limited, so we need to expose ourselves to the new things to feel the wonderful of life.

A: What is your least favorite job?

B: I do not like the work of scientific research. In my opinion, this kind of job is boring. Compared with doing scientific research, communicating with people is more interesting. Just like the old saying, traveling is better than reading ten thousand books. Journey is not as good as reading countless people.

A: How long will you stay with our airline? What kind of contributions will you make to our airline?

B: First of all, I have to say I love this profession, so I would like to devote all to this career till I cannot contribute anything to this job. I will manage to fulfill my duties without any complain.

A: What would your classmates say about you?

B: My classmates say I am reliable, because I will fulfill all the promises that I made. I will not make a promise if I cannot do that. They also think I am an easy-going person, because I put myself in other's position when I deal with problems. I can make friends with different kind of people.

A：你为什么想要成为一名空中乘务员？做一名空中乘务员最好的地方是什么？

B：空中乘务员是我最喜欢的工作之一，它可以带我到世界各地去领略不同的当地文化，带我去见识一些我从没有见识过的东西。而且还可以遇到各行各业、形形色色的人，与人交流是我最喜欢的事情之一。因为人生有限，要在有限的生命里去见识更多的新鲜事物，才能感受到生活的精彩。

A：你最不喜欢的工作是什么？

B：我不太喜欢从事科学研究之类的工作，在我看来这种工作是枯燥乏味的，相比之下我觉得与人打交道更有意思。古语说得好，读万卷书不如行万里路，行万里路不如阅人无数。

A：你打算在我们航空公司干多久？你将为我们公司做出什么贡献呢？

B：首先我要说我爱这个职业，所以我会为了这个职业奉献我所有的一切，直到我不能再为我的工作付出的一天，直到你们不需要我的那一天。我会尽心尽力做好我的分内事，我只会感谢这个公司给我了这个工作而不会有任何抱怨。

A：你的同学是怎么谈论你的？

B：我的同学都说我是一个可以信赖的人。因为，我一旦答应别人的事情，就一定会做到。如果我做不到，我就不会轻易许诺。而且他们觉得我是一个比较随和的人，我在处理问题时，总是能站在别人的角度考虑问题，与不同的人都可以友好相处。

Dialogue 2

A: In your opinion, what will be the biggest challenge of being a flight attendant?

B: The biggest challenge of being a flight attendant is the willingness to serve others and devote yourself. A flight attendant must provide the best service to the passengers and improve the image of the company, so he or she can bring more benefits to the enterprise.

A: Do you consider yourself a team player?

B: Yes, I have the spirit of a team player. I believe collective strength will be stronger than personal strength. To some extent, people can be inspired by unity to make much more effort in work without boring. This is why I should cooperate with the people around me.

A: What kind of people do you prefer to work with?

B: I hope the one whom I work with has a good attitude toward life. He or she should be honest, open-minded, kindhearted, and easy to get along with, so we can make progress together. I believe when you touch black, you become black, when you touch red, you become red.

A: How long do you plan to stay here?

B: I really want to obtain a permanent job. I won't leave as long as I have opportunity to apply my knowledge and get on well with my superiors and colleagues.

A: What are your future plans and what kind of expectations do you have of the company?

B: I know that generally it is possible to move from this position to a management position with two years' experience in the company and I would look forward to having the responsibility for training and supervising new members of staff.

A：你认为，作为一名空中乘务员最大的挑战是什么？

B：作为一个空中乘务员最大的挑战是能否真正拥有愿意为人服务，愿意奉献的精神。作为一个乘务员就要为乘客提供最上乘的服务，完善公司形象，为公司带来更多的利益。

A：你觉得你是一个具有团队精神的人吗？

B：是的，我是一个具有团队精神的人，正所谓众人拾柴火焰高，我相信集体的力量要比每个人单独的力量加起来还要大，因为团结在某种程度上能激励人们更努力地工作，却让人不觉得乏味，这就是人与人之间为什么要合作的原因。

A：你喜欢跟什么样的人共事？

B：我希望跟我一起工作的人能有积极的人生态度。他或她应该诚实、开朗、热心，易于相处，这样大家在一起工作才能共同进步，我相信近朱者赤近墨者黑！

A：你打算在这里工作多久？

B：我很想拥有一个固定的工作，只要我有施展才能的机会，而且能和上级、同事相处得好，我就不会离开。

A：你将来有什么计划？你对公司有什么期望？

B：我知道，通常情况下在贵公司具有了两年的工作经验后是有可能从现在的职位升到管理的位置。我希望能承担培训和监督新员工的职责。

Dialogue 3

A: Tell me about yourself and your past experience.

B: For the past 3 years, I have been working in Air China Limited. I'm very tolerant of people and have been told that this is one of my strengths. I feel I have a lot to offer as a team member.

A: Why are you interested in this occupation?

B: It's always been my dream to be a stewardess. And I like travelling to different places.

A: What do you think is the chief characteristic for a stewardess?

B: Well, a stewardess should be friendly, courteous, patient and treat passengers kindly and politely.

A: If a passenger had an accident, what would you do?

B: I would give him or her basic first aid and ask my partner to call for assistance at the same time.

A: If you are hired, when can you start work?

B: I can begin to work right away because I am out of work now.

A: What are your salary expectations?

B: I really need more information about the job before we start to discuss salary. I'd like to postpone that discussion until later. Maybe you could tell me what is budgeted for the position and how your commission structure works.

A: 说说你自己和你的经历。

B: 过去三年我一直在中国国际航空公司工作。我待人宽容，别人都说这是我的优点。我想作为团队一员，我能做出很多贡献。

A: 你为什么对这个职业感兴趣？

B: 成为一名空姐一直是我的梦想，而且我喜欢到各地旅游。

A: 对空姐来说，你认为主要应该具备的品质是什么？

B: 空姐应该待人友好、有礼貌、有耐心，对乘客和蔼、彬彬有礼。

A: 如果有乘客发生意外，你会怎么办？

B: 我会为他／她做基本的急救，同时让同伴寻求救助。

A: 如果你被录用，什么时候你能开始工作？

B: 为我目前没有工作，所以随时都可以。

A: 你希望拿多少薪水？

B: 在讨论薪水前，我需要更多了解这份工作。我希望迟点讨论这个问题，或者你可以告诉我这个职位的预算薪酬是多少，贵公司的佣金制度是如何运作的。

Dialogue 4

A: Why do you choose to be a stewardess?

B: Well, when I was a little girl, I always lie on the grass, watching the sky, and I envied the birds because they could fly in the blue sky. Therefore, when I grew old, I hope to be a stewardess who can fly in the sky like a bird. That's why I am here for this interview.

A: Do you know the responsibilities of a stewardess?

B: The most important responsibility of a stewardess is to make the passengers feel relaxed and happy during the flight by providing good services.

A: If the passenger cannot understand what you say, what will you do?

B: If he or she cannot understand what I say, I think I will try my best to use gesture or write them down on a paper.

A: Why do you want to be a part of our organization?

B: I think it will be a mutually beneficial relationship. I think the company and I have a lot to offer each other.

A: Can you convince us to employ you?

B: First, I think I have the professional knowledge about how to be a stewardess. Second, I am patient, easygoing, conversable, and positive, all these can help me deal with the problems between passengers and me. Third, I am eager to learn new knowledge. I am a hard worker and will perform to the best of my ability.

A: How long would you like to stay with our company?

B: How long I will stay with the company depends on whether the company and I are satisfied with each other.

A: What do you think of this industry's outlook in five years?

B: I do believe this industry will be developed rapidly in 5 years' time.

A：你为什么要选择做一名空姐？

B：当我还是个小女孩的时候，我总是躺在草地上，看着天空，我羡慕那些鸟儿，因为它们可以在蓝天上飞翔。因此，当我长大的时候，我希望能成为一名空姐，能像鸟儿一样在空中飞翔。这就是我来这里参加这次面试的原因。

A：你知道作为一名乘务员的责任所在吗？

B：空姐最重要的职责是提供良好的服务，让乘客在飞行过程中感到放松和快乐。

A：如果乘客听不懂你说的话，你会怎么做？

B：如果他或她听不懂我说的话，我想我会尽力用手势或把它们写在纸上。

A：你为什么想成为我们组织的一部分？

B：我认为这将是一种互惠互利的关系。我认为公司和我有很多东西可以互相提供。

A：你能说服我们雇用你吗？

B：首先，我想我有如何成为一名空姐的专业知识。其次，我有耐心、随和、健谈、积极，这些都能帮助我解决乘客和我之间的问题。第三，我渴望学习新的知识。我是一个勤劳的人，会尽我最大的努力去工作。

A：你打算在本公司干多长时间？

B：我在贵公司干多长时间取决于我和公司之间是否互相满意。

A：你认为五年内这个行业前景如何？

B：我相信在这五年中，这个行业会迅猛发展的。

Dialogue 5

A: Does your present employer know you are looking for another job?

B: No, I haven't discussed my career plans with my present employer, but I am sure he will understand.

A: Do you think your English can be understood easily by others?

B: Yes, in most circumstances.

A: Are you available for travel?

B: Yes, I like traveling. I am young and unmarried. It's no problem for me to travel frequently.

A: How about overtime work?

B: Overtime work is very common in companies. I can work overtime if it's necessary.

A: Do you like regular work?

B: No, I don't like regular work. I am interested in different projects with new opportunities and new challenge, but I can do regular work if the company needs me to do so.

A: What was your favorite job? Why do you want to be a flight attendant?

B: Stewardess is one of my favorite jobs. This job can take me to different parts of the world to experience the local culture, to see new things that I have never known, to meet different kinds of people in different careers and so on. As we known, the life is limited, so we need to expose ourselves to the new things to feel wonderful of life.

A: How long will you stay with our airline? What kind of contributions will you make to our airline?

B: First of all, I have to say I love this profession, so I would like to devote all to this career till I cannot contribute anything to this job. I will manage to fulfill my duties without any complain.

A: How soon can you begin working for us?

B: I need about two to three weeks for necessary formalities. I will quit then transfer to your company.

A：你现在的老板知道你正在找别的工作吗？

B：他不知道，我还没有跟我现在的老板讨论我的职业计划。但是我想他会理解我的。

A：你觉得你说英语别人容易懂吗？

B：我想在大多数情况下是的。

A：你能出差吗？

B：是的，我还年轻也没有结婚。对我来说经常出差不成问题。

A：那加班呢？

B：在各个公司里加班是很正常的。如果必要的话，我可以加班。

A：你喜欢有规律的工作吗？

B：不，我不喜欢。我对能提供新的机会和挑战的各种不同的工作项目感兴趣。但是如果公司需要的话，我也可以做有规律的工作。

A：你最喜欢的工作是什么？你为什么想要当一名空中乘务员？

B：空中乘务员就是我最喜欢的工作之一，它可以带我到世界各地去领略不同的当地文化，带我去见识一些我从没有见识过的东西。而且还可以遇到各行各业、形形色色的人，等等。正如我们所知，人生有限，所以我们要在有限的生命里去见识更多新鲜的事物，才能感受到精彩的生活。

A：你会在我们航空公司做多久？你又能为航空公司做出什么贡献呢？

B：首先我要说我爱这个职业，所以我会为了这个职业奉献我所有的一切，直到我不能再为我的工作付出的那一天。我会尽心尽力做好我的分内事而不会有任何抱怨。

A：你最快能什么时候开始到我们这工作呢？

B：我需要两到三周的时间去办理必要的手续，之后就能辞职来您这报道、工作了。

Dialogue 6

A: What made you decide on this type of occupation?

B: Oh, to tell you the truth, I love the sky. When I was a child, I imagined flying into the blue sky someday. Now, I think the day has come. My dream will come true. I like travelling very much and I enjoy working with people.

A: Are you a goal-oriented person?

B: Yes, I am. I always make a plan before I do anything.

A: Where do you want to be in 5 years?

B: I don't want to have a specific title. I just want to enjoy what I am doing.

A: That sounds very reasonable.

B: It's the most important thing to me.

A: Do you consider yourself a loyal employee?

B: If I really love the career I choose, I will be one of the most loyal employees in the enterprise. I will put all my energy into the work and devote my life to the company.

A: If you are hired, how long do you plan to stay with us?

B: That obviously depends on how things go—whether I'm suited to the firm and the firm to me.

A: Tell me about some of your recent goals and what you do to achieve them.

B: I want to put my knowledge and experience to use in a challenging position. In order to achieve this goal, I just want to work step by step.

A: What is your long-term objective?

B: I haven't thought it over at all.

A: What do you think is the most important thing when looking for a job?

B: I think the most important thing is the interest in the job.

A：什么原因使你决定投身这个行业呢？

B：哦，说真的，我非常喜欢蓝天。小时候我就梦想自己有一天能飞上蓝天，现在我想这一天已经到了，我的梦想要实现了。我非常喜欢旅游，喜欢和人打交道。

A：你是一个有明确目标的人吗？

B：是的，我是，在做每件事之前我都会做一个计划。

A：你在五年内希望做到什么位置？

B：我并不想要什么特别的头衔，我只想做我喜欢做的事情。

A：听起来非常有道理。

B：这对我来说是最重要的。

A：你觉得你是一个忠诚的员工吗？

B：当我真正喜欢上一个职业的时候，我会是这个企业里最忠诚的员工之一。我会把我所有的精力投入工作当中去，我会把我的一生奉献给这个企业。

A：如果你被录用，计划在我们公司干多久？

B：这当然依事情的发展而定，得看我和公司之间是否互相适合。

A：能说说你的近期目标以及如何去实现它吗？

B：我想把我的知识和经验运用到一个具有挑战性的工作中，为了达到这个目标，我只想一步一步地踏实工作。

A：你的长远目标是什么？

B：我还没有认真考虑过。

A：在找工作时，你认为什么最重要？

B：我认为是对工作的兴趣。

Part V Tips

有时候面试中面试官会提问面试者有关工作目标的问题，目的就是了解面试者做事的风格，以及面试者对这份工作的看法。当然由于面试者还不是很了解自己所应聘的工作，在回答问题时并不一定面面俱到，因为在实际中会碰到自己计划中没有考虑到的问题，所以大致说明自己的计划目标就好了。

"你为什么对我们公司工作感兴趣？"

此问题主要考察应聘者是否了解这个工作，或者是否真正有兴趣，面试官试图从中了解你求职的动机、愿望以及对此项工作的态度。所以应聘者需要围绕整个公司的具体情况对面试官提出的问题进行回答，让面试官知道你很清楚这个公司的运营模式，以及对这项工作非常积极。如果能有一些实际回答的话，加分会更多。在回答这类问题时，建议从行业、企业和岗位这三个角度来回答。如："我十分看好贵公司所在的行业，我认为贵公司十分重视人才，而且这项工作很适合我，相信自己一定能做好。""我来应聘是因为我相信自己能为公司做出贡献，而且我的适应能力使我确信我能把职责带上一个新的台阶。"同时也要注意，不要让面试官觉得你是为了讨好面试官而言过其实。

如今跳槽已是一个很普遍的现象，原因是多种多样的。面试者当被问及跳槽的原因时要把握住一点，那就是你要说出现在应聘的这个公司能为你提供原公司不能提供的方面，包括个人发展、计划、工作环境，等等。

面试官希望知道面试者是否从事过与当前职位相关的工作，或者面试者从以往的工作中吸取到了哪些有用的经验。即便过去的工作和现在应聘的职位无关，也不能说是什么都没有学到，因为每份工作都有它可取之处。有时也许由于种种原因，面试者跳槽比较多，但这不一定是坏事，所以如果自己是属于这种情况，可以向面试官说明干过多种工作使自己经验丰富，能为公司提供更好的服务。

如果面试官问："你为什么辞掉上一份工作？"应聘者可能回想起跳槽的原因是因为上一份工作非常糟糕，但面试并不是适合抱怨的场合，而且千万不要对现有或是过去的雇主或同事进行诋毁性的评论，而要从自身发展的角度出发来回答面试官提出的问题。总之，要让面试官知道，以前的公司在你的眼中并非一钱不值，你是怀着感激来评价他们的。

如果面试官问："我们为什么要录用你？"应聘者在回答此类问题时，最好站在招聘单位的角度来回答。招聘单位一般会录用这样的应聘者：基本符合条件、对这份工作感兴趣、有足够的信心。如"我符合贵公司的招聘条件，凭我目前掌握的技能，自身高度的责任感和良好的适应能力及学习能力，我认为自己完全能胜任这份工作。我十分希望能为贵公司服务，如果贵公司给我这个机会，我一定能成为贵公司的栋梁！"

如果面试官问："如果我们雇佣你，你将在我们公司待多久？"老板想知道你会不会像离开上一份工作那样很快也离开这家公司，你可以告诉老板，你是希望同公司一起成长，不会轻易地离开。

在回答"如果我录用你，你将怎样开展工作"这类问题时，如果你对于应聘的职位缺乏足够的了解，最好不要直接说出自己开展工作的具体办法；可以尝试采用迂回战术来回答，如"首先听取领导的指示和要求，然后就有关情况进行了解和熟悉，接下来制定一份近期的工作计划并报领导批准，最后根据计划开展工作。"

"你如何看待自己在公司内的发展？"

这类问题涉及未来、你的目标以及你计划如何实现这些目标。在面试问题中，它经常被用作一种动机性问题，以评估你对相关职位的付出。不幸的是，这种类型的问题是许多应聘者经常难以有效处理的。在许多情况下，应聘者要么祈祷不会遇上这个问题，要么没有充分考虑到你的未来与公司的潜在发展。因此，应聘者给出的答案通常是临场发挥，这可能会导致整体面试表现降低。

你对这个问题的回答可以根据你对未来的计划采取多种形式进行回答。要记住，面试官想要的答案是把你的计划与你的职位和工作联系起来。当你思考答案的时候，你要确保你为自己规划好了一条清晰简洁的职业道路。例如，你可以展示你未来五年的计划，以及你计划如何把它们与这个职位联系在一起来实现。你也应该展示你的职业发展方向，以及你想要在这个职位上如何发展自己的事业。

通常，当你花了时间去了解公司的情况、公司的组织结构以及它的未来发展计划时，这个问题往往能得到最好的回答。这将使你能够规划一条符合公司各项计划的职业道路，并表明了你已经主动去研究公司和它的目标。不要忽视这个问题的重要性。这个问题确实与未来有关，但是当你的其他表现与其他候选人不分伯仲时，它可能是一个决定成败的问题。

"什么让你遵循你所选择的这条职业道路？"

应聘者在回答此类评判你动机的问题时，关键在选择一个职业或者决定为什么要选择这个职业是发生在面试之前的事情。所以一定要有所准备。这也能帮助你找到一份你喜欢的工作。当你面试空乘这一职位时的时候，不妨说"我喜欢旅游，我喜欢跟人打交道。当有一天我发现，有一种职业能让我在各个地方飞来飞去，又能够接触不同的人时，我想我就一定要从事这个职业了。"又或者"我的父母告诉我要尝试不同的东西，这样的话才能发现我真正喜欢的是什么。毕竟一周大部分的时间都在工作，所以这份工作必须是我喜欢的。在我十几、二十岁的时候，我用做兼职的方式尝试了各种不同类型的工作，我发现，我最想要做的就是飞向蓝天。我一直用这个梦想激励着自己，要刻苦、要努力，所以，今天，我站在了这里。"

在回答完这类问题后，可能还会有类似"为了从事这个职业，你已经做出了哪些努力"的问题，所以，请务必准备好确切的事例来说明你之前在这方面取得了什么成就以及你未来的目标，等等。

"你的目标是什么？"

应聘者回答此类问题时，要避免提到与职业无关的事情。只要你能把事业的成功和家庭的成功联系起来,谈论家庭也是可以的。比如"我要养家,这就意味着我需要一个成功的事业。我要努力工作,这样我才能同公司一起成长、一同发展,这样我才能给我的家人营造一个稳定的家庭环境。"

回答这个问题最糟糕的答案之一就是"我的目标就是数年后坐上你的位置。"同样的目标可以换一种更加积极的方式来表达,比如"我要努力工作,希望公司变得更加成功,在您升职之后,我希望我能坐上您的位置,问坐在我现在这个位置的人同样的问题。"

充分的准备对你回答此类问题会有所帮助。在面试之前就要搞清楚自己的目标,把它们写下来,列出一个清单,然后把这个清单跟工作职位描述和你通过研究了解的公司的相关信息进行比对。如果你能说出你计划达成这些目标所用的方法,这个回答就更加完美了。

比如:在工作中学习,与公司共同成长。"这是一个可以更多了解这份职业的地方,我可以在团队工作中自我成长,同时使公司取得更大成功。"

成为管理人员。"当我获得了足够多的敬仰之后,我想要从事管理工作。"

竞争力。"我想象自己是这样一家公司的优秀员工。为了实现这个目标,我将努力工作,倾听他人的经验,并努力参与公司的相关工作。"

Part VI Supplementary Reading

A: Brief Introduction about Air China Limited

Air China Limited (simplified Chinese: 中国国际航空公司 ; literally: China International Airlines Company) is the flag carrier and one of the major airlines of the People's Republic of China, with its headquarters in Shunyi District, Beijing. Air China's flight operations are based in Beijing Capital International Airport.

History

Air China was established and commenced operations on 1 July, 1988 as a result of the Chinese government's decision in late 1987 to split the operating divisions of Civil Aviation Administration of China (CAAC) into six separate airlines: Air China, China Eastern, China Southern, China Northern, China Southwest, and China Northwest. Air China was given chief responsibility for intercontinental flights and took over the CAAC's long haul aircraft (Boeing 747s, 767s, and 707s) and routes.

In January, 2001, the former CAAC's ten airlines agreed on a merger plan, according to which Air China was to acquire China South West Airlines. Before the acquisition, Air China was the country's fourth largest domestic airline. The merger created a group with assets of 56 billion Yuan (USD $8.63 billion), and a fleet of 118 aircrafts. In October 2002, Air China consolidated with the China National Aviation Corporation and China Southwest Airlines.

On 15 December, 2004, Air China was successfully listed on the Hong Kong and London Stock Exchanges. The airline also listed its shares on the Shanghai Stock Exchange on 18 August, 2006.

In 2006, Air China signed an agreement to join the Star Alliance. It became a member of the alliance on 12 December, 2007 alongside Shanghai Airlines.

In April 2010, Air China completed the increase of shareholdings in Shenzhen Airlines and became the controlling shareholder of Shenzhen Airlines, allowing Air China to further enhance its position in Beijing, Chengdu, and Shanghai as well as achieve a more balanced domestic network.

On 23 December, 2010, Air China became the first Chinese airline to offer combined tickets that include domestic flights and shuttle bus services to nearby cities. The first combined flight-shuttle bus ticket connected Tianjin via shuttle bus with domestic flights passing through Beijing.

Air China began offering Wi-Fi internet service on board its aircraft on 15 November, 2011, making it the first Chinese carrier to offer this service.

In early 2015, it was announced that the airline had selected the Boeing 737 Next Generation and 737MAX for its fleet renewal program of 60 aircrafts. The deal, with a value of over $6B at current list prices, has yet to be finalized.

Corporate Affairs

The entity Air China Limited was registered in 2003, and its shares began trading in Hong Kong and London on December 15, 2004. Originally the airline corporate entity was Air China International, which was founded in 2002. Air China International incorporated China Southwest Airlines and the air transportation services of the China National Aviation Company, becoming a new entity. As of June 2015, it ranks No. 1 of Chinese companies for long-term accounts payable. The enterprise logo of Air China consists of an artistic phoenix pattern, the name of the airline written in calligraphy by former national leader Deng Xiaoping, and "AIR CHINA" in English. The phoenix logo is also the artistic transfiguration of the word "VIP". Air China is a member of the Star Alliance.

Destinations

Air China's route network extends throughout Asia to the Middle East, Western Europe, and North America from its main hub at Beijing Capital International Airport. It also currently reaches a significant number of Asian, Australian and European destinations from Shanghai. Some international routes operate from Chengdu, Chongqing, Dalian, Hangzhou, Kunming and Xiamen. It is one of the few world airlines that fly to all six inhabitable continents.

Frequent Flyer Program

Phoenix Miles (Chinese: 凤凰知音; literally: Phoenix Concert), is the frequent flyer program of Air China. This is the first frequent flyer program launched in China. It was designed to reward frequent flyers traveling internationally and domestically with Air China and its partner airlines.

B: Flight Safety Instructions

When traveling by air, following certain safety precautions can help your flight go more smoothly and reduce the risk of danger, should an emergency situation arise. Airlines typically provide both printed and verbal safety instructions at the start of each flight.

Baggage

How and where you stow your carry-on baggage during a flight is a matter of flight safety. Any baggage stored in overhead compartments should fit appropriately, so that compartment doors latch securely. Baggage stored underneath the seat should not protrude, as any items underfoot might impede a quick exit in the case of an emergency. Should evacuation prove necessary, leave all your baggage behind?

Electronics

The use of electronic devices on board an aircraft is subject to limitations by the Federal Aviation Administration and the Federal Communications Commission. Use of cellular phones, for example, can interfere with important signaling devices used in the cockpit. For this reason, cellphones, radios and hand-held televisions are all prohibited during the flight. Cellular phones must be turned off or to a "airplane" setting during the duration of the flight. Use of laptops and other personal electronic devices is permissible at certain points during the flight. Flight attendants will signal when passengers are allowed to use them.

Emergency Procedures

If the cabin air pressure changes dramatically, oxygen masks might fall from the ceiling directly in front of you. Follow the airline's instructions in operating their masks. If a child is seated beside you, put on your own mask before helping to put a mask on the child. Should an emergency arise that requires you to evacuate the airplane, follow the lighting on the aisle or over the seats to the nearest exit. Follow any instructions you receive from flight attendants and remain calm. If you are sitting in an emergency exit row, you might need to perform extra actions, such as opening the emergency door. If you must evacuate along a slide, take off any high-heeled shoes before getting on the slide. Once you have evacuated the aircraft, move away from it. Never return to a burning aircraft.

General Safety Procedures

Each time that you fly, consult the safety information card provided by your airline for any variations or changes in the recommended safety procedures. Look for the exit closest to your seat, noting that the nearest exit might be behind you and counting the number of rows between your seat and the exit. Only sit in an emergency exit row if you are capable of following the extra emergency actions. Locate the flotation device, typically beneath your seat.

C: About Airbus

Airbus is an international pioneer in the aerospace industry. We are a leader in designing, manufacturing and delivering aerospace products, services and solutions to customers on a global scale. We aim for a better-connected, safer and more prosperous world.

A commercial aircraft manufacturer, with Space and Defense as well as Helicopters Divisions, Airbus is the largest aeronautics and space company in Europe and a worldwide leader.

Airbus has built on its strong European heritage to become truly international—with roughly 180 locations and 12,000 direct suppliers globally. The company has aircraft and helicopter final assembly lines across Asia, Europe and the Americas, and has achieved a more than six fold order book increase since 2000.

Innovation has always been a driving force at Airbus, which promotes cutting-edge technologies and scientific excellence to contribute to global progress. Through its predecessor companies, Airbus pioneered many of the technologies that helped conquer the skies and are now part of everyday life.

Airbus encourages its industry-leading experts to push their boundless imaginations, moving the company into the Industry 4.0 era and inventing new possibilities for the future of flight: from manned and unmanned vehicles for urban mobility, to hybrid and electric propulsion systems for cleaner aviation.

Around 130 nationalities make up the Airbus workforce. By 2020, 25% of its employees will be women, underlining its commitment to a diverse and inclusive workforce. Airbus also recognizes engagement and a strong leadership culture, headed by its CEO Tom Enders.

Looking beyond its own resources, Airbus is a signatory of the UN Global Compact and its work contributes to the Sustainable Development Goals. The company's people and equipment also help bring aid to disaster zones, and through the Airbus Foundation it is educating and inspiring youngsters, ensuring future generations of innovative scientists and engineers.

Unit 4
如何应对专业问答——
展现技能水平

Part I Introduction

在航空公司面试时，除了注重外形的初试以外，后续的复试都有评委问答环节。不仅是航空公司的面试，在其他民航类企业的面试过程中，面试官也大都会向应聘者发问，而应聘者的回答将成为面试官考虑是否接受你的重要依据。应聘者在这个问答环节本就容易紧张，那么英文面试问答更是愁坏不少应聘者，所以，提前了解这些问题的考核点，做到胸有成竹，至关重要。

其实英文面试并不难，受限于面试者甚至考官的英文水平，大部分英文面试的题目比较固定，并且都是不会探讨太深的问题。

面试的英文问答大致分为语言表达类问题，应聘动机与期望类问题，观察事业心、进取心和自信心类问题，观察工作态度、组织纪律性类问题，以及考察应变能力类问题。语言表达类问题多为自我介绍，主要观察应聘者的语言是否流畅、有条理、层次分明，讲话的风度如何。"你为什么选择来我公司工作？"这是一道典型的观察应聘动机与期望的面试问答题，如果你只为找到一份工作糊口而盲目求职，那么，公司会认为你的培养潜质不高，所以说，在面试前，一定要对公司有一定的了解。除了常规问题以外，有时面试官还会抛出一些难以回答的问题来考察你的应变能力。在回答这种问题时，一定要记住，面试官的考核点在于应聘者的反馈时间，一定要在 20 秒内进行回答。

除了这些个人问答以外，面试时也避免不了会出现考核应聘者技能水平的专业问题。有时候，这些专业问题会成为面试成功的最基本要素。在面试前，一定要先审视一下自身的知识掌握程度，如果有必要，可以利用空闲时间系统地再学习一遍，多多复习相关的民航专业单词、对话及机上广播词，千万不要没有一点知识储备就跑去面试，不要眼睁睁地看着自己心仪的工作机会擦肩而过。

Part II Glossary

	New Words
route	*n.* 路线；航线
province	*n.* 省；领域
locate	*vi.* 定位
distance	*n.* 距离

New Words	
limit	*n.* 限制；限度；界线
economic	*adj.* 经济的
volume	*n.* 量；体积
exclude	*vt.* 排除；排斥
domestic	*adj.* 国内的
airfare	*n.* 飞机票价
infant	*adj.* 婴儿的
accompanied	*adj.* 伴随的；相伴的
signal	*n.* 信号；暗号
exit	*n.* 出口
pet	*n.* 宠物
blind	*adj.* 盲目的；瞎的
temperature	*n.* 温度；体温
pregnant	*adj.* 怀孕的
manufacturer	*n.* 制造商
stewardess	*n.* 空姐，乘务员
abbreviation	*n.* 缩写；缩写词
association	*n.* 协会，联盟，社团
code	*n.* 代码，密码
phoenix	*n.* 凤凰
swallow	*n.* 燕子
kapok flower	*n.* 木棉花
Useful Phrases	
refer to	参考；涉及；指的是；适用于
according to	根据
checked luggage	托运行李
fresh water lake	淡水湖
cruising speed	巡行航速

Part III Q&A

1. What is the mountain on the route from Beijing to Shanghai? Taishan Mountain or Baiyun Mountain?

   Taishan Mountain.

2. What is the mountain on the route from Beijing to Guangzhou? Liang Mountain or Luoxiao Mountain?

   Luoxiao Mountain.

3. What is the mountain on the route from Beijing to Kunming? Taihang Mountain or Wutai Mountain?

   Taihang Mountain.

4. Is Hongze Lake the biggest fresh water lake in China or the third biggest fresh water lake in China?

   The third biggest fresh water lake in China.

5. Which is the biggest fresh water lake in China? Tai Lake or Boyang Lake.

   Boyang Lake.

6. Does Guizhou Province locate in China's south mountain area or Yungui Plateau?

   Yungui Plateau.

7. Does Shaanxi Province locate in Huanghe River's middle reaches area or upper reaches area?

   In Huanghe River's middle reaches area.

8. Is Yangzi River the longest river in China or the second longest river in China?

   The longest river in China.

9. Where does Huanghe River rise? From Qinghai Plateau or the north part of Bayankala Mountain in Qinghai Province?

   The north part of Bayankala Mountain in Qinghai Province.

10. How far is the flight distance from Beijing to Shanghai? 1160km or 2000km.

    1160km.

11. How far is the flight distance from Beijing to Dalian? 607km or 800km.

    607km.

12. How far is the flight distance from Beijing to Shenzhen? 2146km or 1960km.

    2146km.

13. What is the name of the airport in Changsha? Changsha Huanghua Airport or Hunan Changsha Airport?

    Changsha Huanghua Airport.

14. What is the cruising speed of an aircraft? Taking off speed or speed after taking off?

    Speed after taking off.

15. Is the weight of the hand baggage for a passenger flying from Beijing to Shanghai 5kg or 10kg?

    5kg.

16. What is the weight limit for economic cabin passenger's free luggage? 30kg or 20kg?
    20kg.

17. What is the weight limit for first cabin passenger's free luggage? 40kg or 20kg?
    40kg.

18. What is the weight limit of each checked luggage? No more than 30kg or no more than 50kg?
    No more than 50kg.

19. What is the volume limit of the checked luggage? Not exclude 50cm × 60cm × 100cm or 40cm × 60cm × 100cm?
    40cm × 60cm × 100cm.

20. How much is the air fare for business cabin on a domestic air service? 130% of the airfare for the economic cabin or 120% of the airfare for the economic cabin?
    130% of the airfare for the economic cabin.

21. How much is the air fare for first cabin on a domestic air service? 200% of the airfare for the economic cabin or 150% of the airfare for the economic cabin?
    150% of the airfare for the economic cabin.

22. How much is an infant airfare? 10% of the adult airfare or 50% of the adult airfare?
    10% of the adult airfare.

23. What does the word "children" refer to when taking aircraft? Children at the age between 2-12, or children at the age between 2-15?
    Children at the age between 2-12.

24. What is the age limit for a no adult accompanied child? Aged from 2-12, or from 5-12?
    From 5-12.

25. What is the signal for no adult accompanied child on the ticket? CHD or UM?
    UM.

26. Who can not sit at the exit seat? Passenger under the age of 15 or under the age of 12?
    Passanger under the age of 15.

27. Whose weight does not include in the free luggage of a passenger? A pet dog or a blind aided dog?
    A blind aided dog.

28. Is the wine served on the flight at the room temperature or iced?
    At the room temperature.

29. In what situation is a pregnant woman not able to take aircraft? She has been in pregnancy for over 6 months or 8 months?
    8 months.

30. For which of the following reasons can an airline refuse to carry the passenger and his or her luggage? Passengers who refuse to accept security checks or request upgrades to their cabins.
    Passengers who refuse to accept security cheeks.

31. What is the color for the onboard passenger life jacket? Yellow or red?
    Yellow.

32. What is the color for the on board aircrew life jacket? Red or yellow?
    Red.

33. Which is the manufacturer of A380? Boeing or Airbus?
    Airbus.

34. Who is the first aircraft manufacturer in China?
    Fengru.

35. Who is the first fire balloon manufacturer in the world?
    Mont brother.

36. What should a stewardess take on his or her duty? Steward certification or employee's card?
    Steward certification.

37. What is the name of Beijing Airport?
    Beijing Capital International Airport.

38. What is the name of Tianjin Airport?
    Tianjin Binhai International Airport.

39. Which is the correct abbreviation for civil aviation administration of China?
    CAAC.

40. What is the English abbreviation of International Air Transport Association?
    IATA.

41. Which is the English code for Muslim Meal? KSML or MOML?
    MOML.

42. Which is the English code for Kosher Meal? KSML or MOML?
    KSML.

43. Which is the English code for Hindu Meal? HNML or MOML?
    HNML.

44. What is the logo of Air China?
    Phoenix.

45. What is the logo of China Eastern Airlines?
    Swallow.

46. What is the logo of China Southern Airlines?
    Kapok flower.

47. Which is the 2 digit code for Air China?
    CA.

48. Which is the 2 digit code for China Southern Airlines?
    CZ.

49. Which is the 2 digit code for China Eastern Airlines?
    MU.

50. Which is the 2 digit code for Xiamen Airlines?
    MF.

51. Which is the 2 digit code for Shanghai Airlines?
    FM.

52. Which is the 2 digit code for Juneyao Airlines?

    HO.

53. Which is the 2 digit code for Sichuan Airlines?

    3U.

54. Which is the 2 digit code for Shenzhen Airlines?

    ZH.

55. Which is the 2 digit code for Shandong Airlines?

    SC.

56. Which is the 2 digit code for Hainan Airlines?

    HU.

57. Which is the 2 digit code for Tianjin Airlines?

    GS.

58. Which is the 2 digit code for Hebei Airlines?

    NS.

59. Which is the 2 digit code for Chengdu Airlines?

    EU.

60. Which is the 2 digit code for Okay Airways?

    BK.

Part IV In-flight Announcement

Baggage Arrangement 引导入座广播

Ladies and Gentlemen,

Welcome aboard _____ Airlines. Please take your seat according to your seat number. Your seat number is on the edge of the rack. Please make sure your hand baggage is stored in the overhead locker. Any small articles can be put under the seat in front of you. Please take your seat as soon as possible to keep the aisle clear for others to go through.

Thank you!

各位女士，各位先生：

欢迎您搭乘_____航空公司的班机旅行，请您对照手中登机牌上的号码对号入座，座位号位于行李架边缘，大件行李请放在行李架上，并请放置稳妥整齐，小件物品建议您放在您前排座椅下方。请您尽快入座，以保持过道通畅，方便其他旅客顺利通过。

谢谢!

Boarding Welcome 欢迎词广播

Good morning / afternoon / evening, Ladies and Gentlemen :

Welcome aboard _____(airlines) flight _____ from _____ to_____. We are flying to _____, the whole flight takes about _____ hours and _____ minutes, and would you please check your ticket and boarding pass again to make sure you're boarding the correct flight.

Thank you!

上午 / 下午 / 晚上好，尊敬的各位女士，各位先生：

欢迎您搭乘坐_____（航空公司）由_____前往_____的_____次航班，到达_____的空中飞行时间为____小时_____分钟。请各位旅客确认您的机票与登机牌，以免误乘航班。

谢谢！

Restriction of Electronic Devices 限制使用电子装置广播

Ladies and Gentlemen,

Welcome aboard _____ Airlines flight _____. Now the cabin door has been closed. To avoid interference with navigation system, please switch off your mobile phones and all electronic devices. Please fasten the seatbelts, ensure that your tables and seatbacks are in an upright position and open the window shades. Smoking is not allowed during the whole flight. We wish you a pleasant trip.

Thank you!

女士们，先生们：

欢迎您乘坐 _____ 航空公司的 _____ 航班。现在舱门已经关闭，为了避免干扰通信导航系统，请您将手机或电子设备全部关闭。请您系好安全带，收起小桌板，调直座椅靠背并打开遮光板。我们提醒各位旅客，本次航班全程禁烟，祝您旅途愉快！

谢谢！

Safety demonstration 安全演示广播

Ladies and Gentlemen,

We will show you the use of life vest, oxygen mask, seatbelt and the location of the emergency exits. Please give us your full attention for the demonstration.

女士们，先生们：

现在乘务员将为您介绍救生衣、氧气面罩、安全带的使用方法和紧急出口的位置，请注意我们的示范和说明。

Your oxygen mask is stored in the compartment above your head, and it will drop automatically in case of emergency. When the mask drops, pull it towards you to cover your mouth and nose, and slip the elastic band over your head, and then breathe normally.

氧气面罩储藏在您头顶上方的壁板里，当发生紧急情况时，面罩会自动脱出，请您用力向下拉面罩，然后将面罩罩在口鼻处，把带子套在头上就可以正常呼吸了。

Each chair has a seatbelt that must be fastened when you are seated. Please keep your seatbelt securely fastened during the whole flight. If needed, you may release the seatbelt by pulling the flap forward. You can adjust it when necessary.

每位旅客座椅上都有一条安全带，请您将安全带扣好并确认。如需要解开，只需要将金属扣向外打开即可。您可以根据需要自行调节长度。

Your life vest is located under your seat. It can only be used in case of ditching. Please do not remove it unless instructed by your flight attendant.

救生衣在您座椅下方的口袋里，仅供水上迫降时使用，在正常情况下请不要取出。

To put your vest on, simply slip it over your head, then fasten the buckles and pull the straps tightly around your waist.

使用时取出，经头部穿好。将带子由后向前在腰间扣好、系紧。

Upon exiting the aircraft, pull the tabs down firmly to inflate your vest; please do not inflate your vest while inside the cabin. For further inflation, simply blow into the mouth pieces on either side of your vest.

当您离开飞机时，拉动救生衣下部的红色充气手柄，但在客舱内不要充气。充气不足时，将救生衣上部的两个充气管拉出，用嘴向里充气。

For ditching at night, a sea-light will be illuminated automatically.

夜间迫降时，救生衣上的指示灯遇水会自动发亮。

There are eight (six) emergency exits. Two in the front of the cabin, two in the rear and four (two) in the middle.

The lights located on the floor will guide you to the exits if an emergency arises. For further information, safety instruction is in the bank pocket of your front seat. Please read it carefully before taking off.

Thank you!

本架飞机客舱内共有 8（6）个紧急出口，前舱 2 个，后舱 2 个，中间 4（2）个。

请不要随意拉动紧急窗口的手柄。客舱通道及出口处都设有紧急照明灯，紧急情况下请按指示灯路线撤离飞机。《安全须知》在您前排座椅背后的口袋里，请您在起飞前仔细阅读。

谢谢！

Pre-flight 起飞前安全检查

Ladies and Gentlemen,

Now, please fasten your seatbelts, stow your tray table, return your footrest to its initial position and put your seat back to the upright position. Please help us by opening the sunshades.

To ensure the safe operation of the navigation system, please make sure your cell phones, including those with flying mode, are switched off.

This is a non-smoking flight, please do not smoke onboard.

We hope you enjoy the flight.

Thank you!

女士们，先生们：

现在，客舱乘务员将进行起飞前的安全确认。请您将安全带系好，收起座椅靠背、小桌板及脚踏板，遮光板保持在打开的状态。

为了避免干扰通讯导航系统的正常工作，请确保您的手机及具有"飞行模式"功能的所有电子设备已经处于关闭状态。

有吸烟习惯的旅客，我们提醒您：本次航班全程禁烟，敬请谅解！

祝您旅途愉快。

谢谢！

Ascending Notice Announcement 飞机上升阶段提示广播

Ladies and Gentlemen,

May I have your attention please!

We are climbing now and we may encounter some turbulence. For your safety, please remain seated and fasten your seat belt. We will serve you soon.

Thank you!

旅客朋友们：

我们的飞机正在上升高度，可能会有颠簸。为了您的安全，请暂时不要离开座位，请您系好安全带。等飞行稳定后，我们将立即为您提供服务。

谢谢！

Introduce the Flight Route 航线介绍广播

Ladies and Gentlemen,

Welcome you aboard _____(airlines) flight _____. (This is the code-share flight with _____ Airlines.)

We have left _____ for _____ (via_____). The distance between _____ and _____ is _____ kilometers. Our flight will take _____ hours and _____ minutes. We expect to arrive at _____ airport at_____.

Along this route, we will be flying over the provinces of _____, passing the cities of_____, crossing over the _____ (river, lake, mountain and ocean).

For your safety, we strongly recommend that you keep your seatbelt fastened at all times, as there may be unexpected turbulence in flight.

Breakfast (lunch / dinner / refreshments / snack) and beverages have been prepared for you. If you need any assistance, please feel comfortable to contact any one of us.

We wish you a pleasant journey. Thank you!

女士们，先生们：

欢迎您乘坐_____航班。本次航班为_____（航空公司）和_____（航空公司）的代码共享航班。

我们的飞机已经离开_____前往_____（途经_____），由_____至_____的飞行距离是_____千米，飞行时间_____小时_____分，预计到达_____机场的时间是_____点_____分。

沿着这条航线，我们将飞经_____（省／直辖市／自治区），经过的主要城市有_____，我们还将飞越_____（海洋、山脉、河流、湖泊）。

在飞行全程中，可能会出现因气流变化引起的突然颠簸，我们特别提醒您，注意系好安全带。

旅途中，我们为您准备了_____（正餐／点心／小吃）及各种饮料。如果您需要帮助，我们很乐意随时为您服务。

旅客朋友们，能为您提供最优质的服务，伴您度过轻松愉快的旅程，是我们全体机组成员的荣幸。谢谢！

Salutatory 行礼广播

Ladies and Gentlemen,

Welcome aboard_____（airlines）. And our cabin crew will spare no effort to provide you with excellent service.

Thank you!

各位女士，各位先生：

欢迎您搭乘_____航班旅行。我们的机组人员将不遗余力地为您提供优质的服务。

谢谢！

Temperature Adjusting 毛毯发放完客舱温度调节广播

Ladies and Gentlemen,

The blankets have been sent out. And we have informed our captain to adjust the cabin temperature. We apologize for any discomfort it may cause. The situation will be improved soon. Thank you!

各位女士，各位先生：

由于目前机上毛毯已经发完，我们已经通知机长调整客舱温度，因此给您带来不适，深表歉意。目前的状况很快就会有所改善。感谢您的理解与配合！

Catering Service 供餐广播

Ladies and Gentlemen,

In a few moments, the flight attendants will be serving meal / snacks and beverages. We hope you will enjoy them.

For the convenience of the passenger seated behind you, please return your seat back to the upright position during our meal service. If you need any assistance, please feel comfortable to contact us. Thank you!

女士们，先生们：

我们将为您提供餐食／点心及各种饮料，希望您能喜欢。在用餐期间，请您调直座椅靠背，以方便后排的旅客。如需要帮助，我们很乐意为您服务。谢谢！

In-flight Entertainment 机上娱乐设备

Ladies and Gentlemen,

For your convenience of travel, we have prepared in-flight entertainment equipment for you. When you finish using it, please put it into the seat pocket in front of you. We wish you a pleasant journey.

女士们、先生们：

为了丰富您的旅途生活，我们在机上为您配备了娱乐设备。您使用完这些设备后，请将其放置于您面前的座椅口袋中。祝您旅途愉快。

In-flight Sales 免税商品销售

Ladies and Gentlemen,

For passengers interested in purchasing Duty Free items, we have a wide selection for sale on this flight. All items are priced in US dollars. Please check with the flight attendant for prices in other currencies. Detailed information can be found in the Duty Free Catalog in the seat pocket in front of you. Thank you!

女士们，先生们：

我们将进行机上免税品销售，我们为您提供多种优质名牌货品，欢迎选购！各种货品均有美元价格。如果您想了解其他货币标价，请咨询乘务员。在您座椅前方的口袋里备有购物指南供您查阅。谢谢！

Comments 意见卡

Ladies and Gentlemen,

Welcome aboard _____ Airlines. Comments from you will be highly valued in order to improve our service. Thanks for your concern and support.

女士们，先生们：

欢迎乘坐_____航班，为了帮助我们不断提高服务质量。敬请留下宝贵意见，谢谢您的关心与支持。

Slight Turbulence 轻度颠簸

Ladies and Gentlemen,

Our aircraft is experiencing some turbulence. Please be seated, fasten your seatbelt. Do not use the lavatories. Please watch out while taking meals.

Thank you!

女士们，先生们：

我们的飞机受气流影响有些颠簸，请您坐好，系好安全带。洗手间暂停使用。正在用餐的旅客，请当心餐饮烫伤或弄脏衣物。

谢谢！

Moderate Turbulence 中度颠簸

Ladies and Gentlemen,

Our aircraft is now experiencing some moderate turbulence, and it will last for some time. (The captain has informed us that we will pass through an area of rough air in _____ minutes; the moderate turbulence will last for _____ minutes.) Please be seated, fasten your seatbelt. Do not use the lavatories. Please watch out while taking meals.

Cabin service will be suspended for a moment.

Thank you!

女士们，先生们：

我们的飞机正经历较强烈的颠簸（接机长通知，大约在_____分钟后，我们的飞机将经过一段气流不稳定区，会有持续的较强烈颠簸）。请您坐好，系好安全带，洗手间暂停使用。正在用餐的旅客，请当心餐饮弄脏衣物。

我们将暂停客舱服务，请您谅解。

谢谢！

Severe Turbulence 重度颠簸

Ladies and Gentlemen,

We have met some severe turbulence, please take your seat and fasten your seatbelts. Do not use the lavatories.

Cabin service will be suspended during this period.

Cabin crew return to your jump seat!

女士们，先生们：

我们的飞机正经历强烈的颠簸，请您尽快就座，系好安全带，洗手间停止使用。

在此期间，我们将暂停客舱服务。

客舱乘务员各就各位！

30 Minutes before Landing 落地前 30 分钟广播

Ladies and Gentlemen,

We will be landing at Peking Capital International Airport in about 30 minutes. Now it is 11:20. The weather is clear and the temperature is 33 degrees centigrade. Please arrange all your belongings in advance. Please return your blankets to the flight attendants.

We are descending now, the lavatory has been suspended. According to the regulations of CAAC, our flight attendants can only carry out safe duty during descent. For your safety, please fasten your seat belt, bring your seat back and table to the upright position, open the window shades. All electronic devices should be turned off.

During descent, your ears may feel uncomfortable because of the changing of cabin pressure. And you can overcome it by swallowing.

Thank you!

女士们，先生们：

飞机将在 30 分钟后到达北京首都国际机场。现在是北京时间 11 点 20 分。目前天气晴朗，地面温度是 33 摄氏度。请您提前整理好随身物品。乘务员将收回毛毯。

女士们，先生们，我们的飞机已经开始下降，洗手间停止使用。根据中国民航局客舱安全管理规定，在此期间，乘务员只能履行安全职责。现在，乘务员将进行客舱安全检查，为了您的安全，请您系好安全带，收起小桌板，调直座椅靠背，坐在靠窗的旅客请您将遮光板打开，关闭手提电脑及所有电子设备。

下降期间，客舱压力会发生变化，如果您感觉耳部不适，可以通过吞咽动作来缓解。
谢谢！

Descending Notice 下降提示广播

Ladies and Gentlemen,

We are descending now and we may encounter some turbulence. For your safety, please sit down and fasten your seat belt.

Thank you!

女士们，先生们：

我们的飞机正在下降，可能会遇到颠簸。为了您的安全，请您不要离开座位，请系好安全带。

谢谢！

Pre-landing 落地前安全检查

Ladies and Gentlemen,

We are beginning our final descent. Please fasten your seatbelts, return your seat back to the upright position and stow your tray table, and return your footrest to its initial position. Please help us by opening the sunshades. All laptop computers and electronic devices should be turned off at this time. We kindly remind you that during landing and taxiing, please keep your seatbelts fastened and do not open the overhead compartment. We will be dimming the cabin lights for landing.

Thank you!

女士们，先生们：

我们的飞机已经开始下降，乘务员将进行安全确认。请您将安全带系好，收起座椅靠背、小桌板及脚踏板，遮光板保持在打开的状态。请您关闭手提电脑及其他电子设备。为了您的安全，在飞机着陆及滑行期间，请不要解开安全带或打开行李架。稍后，我们将调暗客舱灯光。

谢谢！

Taxiing 滑行提示广播

Ladies and Gentlemen,

The plane has arrived at its destination airport. The Fasten Seat Belt Sign will remain illuminated while the plane is taxiing. Please remain seated with your seat belt fastened.

Please take all your carry-on items with you when you disembark and make sure no personal belongings are left in the seat pocket in front of you. When the plane comes to a complete stop, please be careful when opening the overhead lockers to prevent articles from falling out. Your baggage can be claimed at the arrival hall.

Thank you for choosing _____ Airlines. We apologize again for the delay. We strive to provide considerate service at all times. We look forward to serving you again in the near future.

See you on your next trip! Thank you!

女士们，先生们：

飞机已经降落在_____机场。在滑行期间，安全带信号灯尚未熄灭，请您不要解开安全带。

下机时请带好您的全部手提物品，并请确认在您前方座椅口袋内没有遗留私人物品。飞机停稳后，请小心开启行李架，以免行李滑落。您托运的行李，下机后请在到达厅行李提取处领取。

感谢您选择_____航班，以及在航班延误期间对我们工作的理解与配合。我们期望很快能再度为您服务。

下次旅途再会！谢谢！

Landing 落地广播

Ladies and Gentlemen,

We have arrived in Xi'an, the distance between Xi'an Xianyang International Airport and downtown is 47 kilometers. It is Beijing Time 15:30. The outside temperature is 28 degrees Centigrade.

We are taxiing now, for your safety, please turned off your mobile phone. In case of disturb communicate between cockpit and control tower, please do not open the overhead locker. When the airplane has come to a complete stop, we will brighten the cabin. Please open the overhead locker carefully, and then you can get ready for disembarkation.

Thank you for flying with _____ Airlines and see you next time!

女士们，先生们：

我们已经到达西安，西安咸阳国际机场距市区 47 千米。现在是北京时间 15 点 30 分，地面温度 28 摄氏度。

现在，飞机还在滑行中，请您不要打开手机电源，以免干扰机组与地面的通信联络。同时，请不要离开座位提取行李，以防止行李滑落砸伤您或周围的旅客。当飞机完全停稳后，我们会调亮客舱灯光提示您，届时请您小心开启行李架提取行李，并整理好所有随身物品准备下飞机。

感谢您选乘_____航空公司的班机，我们期待着与您再一次相聚。

After Open the Door Reminder 下机提醒广播

Ladies and Gentlemen,

Our airplane has arrived assigned position. Before leaving, please check to take all our carry-on baggage. Thank you!

女士们，先生们：

现在飞机已经完全停稳。请您下飞机时确认是否已经带齐了所有的随身物品。谢谢！

Waiting for Boarding Bridge (Shuttle Bus / Ramp) 等待廊桥（摆渡车 / 客梯车）

Ladies and Gentlemen,

We are still waiting for the boarding bridge (shuttle bus / ramp). Please remain seated, and we will inform you to disembark as soon as the air bridge arrives.

Thank you for your understanding. Thank you!

女士们，先生们：

由于_____机场繁忙的原因，机场廊桥（摆渡车／客梯车）还未到达，请您在座位上稍作休息，待廊桥到达后我们将立即安排您下机。

不便之处，敬请谅解，谢谢！

Part V　Supplementary Reading

A: What should a flight attendant do when a flight is delayed ?

On a flight from Beijing to Xi'an, the plane was delayed due to the bad weather condition. At this time, stewardess Li found an elder passenger sitting in her seat, weeping softly. She walked over and asked what had happened. The old lady said that she was travelling to Guiyang by plane for the first time and had to switch flights in Xi'an. She was so worried about failing to catch the transit plane. After that, Li comforted the elder, and then completed a series of related work. Finally, the old lady boarded the plane on time with a smile.

The main adverse consequence of flight delays is the missing of the transit flight. Flight attendants should record the number of flights, departure time and the number of passengers, then report the captain to inform the ground staff, trying to help passengers quickly handle the transfer procedures. At the same time, if there is some information that the ground security department requires the passengers to understand, the crew should also broadcast them back to the passengers. In addition, transit passengers have priority. Flight attendants can provide some advice according to the flight schedule, but should not make any promise to the passengers.

B: What will you do if a passenger is still asleep when the plane is descending ?

The plane began to decline. The flight attendant found that a passenger was sleeping. She didn't want to disturb the passenger, so she pressed the button to adjust the seat back with one hand and lifted the chair back gently with the other one, wanting to put the seat back in the upright position. But unfortunately, the passenger was awakened by her. "What are you doing?" he shouted, "you should tell me! You scared me out of my wits!" The flight attendant hastened to apologize. The passenger frowned without a word.

Do not look down upon any small part of the service. In this case, the flight attendant did it all out of kindness; however, she had offended the passenger. If the crew found that a passenger was asleep during descending, you could temporarily not disturb him and asked the passengers sitting next to him to tell him to adjust the seatback when he woke up. Five minutes before landing, the crew should check again. If the passenger was still sleeping, you must wake him, and please mind your words.

C: Why couldn't the flight attendants offer the headsets before departure ?

On a recent flight to Changsha, a passenger asked the flight attendant for a pair of headsets before departure. "The plane will take off shortly. After that, we will offer you the headsets." Flight attendant explained with a smile. Shortly after the take-off, the seatbelt sign had not been switched off yet, the passenger pressed the call button again. Flight attendant stepped forward unsteadily because the flight really bumped. "Miss, do you really want to give me the headsets? You are making the excuse for not working. I want to complain!" The passenger said angrily. Flight attendant saw his frown and hastened to explain. Finally he understood.

After the plane had just taken off, it was still in the key phase of the flight. The seatbelt signs haven't been turned off and the plane was inclined. It was not safe for the crew members and passengers to stand or walk in the cabin. The safety should be the priority for a civil aircraft. The relationship between security and service must be handled well. The best service is safety. On the basis of safety, flight attendants should do their best to fulfill passengers' requirements with care, try not to keep them waiting. Improving the service is the fundamentals of airlines management.

参 考 文 献

［1］杰·布洛克，迈克尔·贝特鲁斯. 求职面试的好问题和好答案［M］. 北京：中国青年出版社，2015.

［2］陈根生，汤平平. 新编航空乘务人员面试英语［M］. 北京：中国经济出版社，2015.

［3］黄华，陆晓赟，王卫平. 空乘求职面试英语［M］. 天津：天津大学出版社，2017.

［4］刘爽. 面试英语口语大全［M］. 北京：机械工业出版社，2014.

［5］金利. 面试英语开口说［M］. 北京：清华大学出版社，2014.

［6］李智允. 全英文面试攻略大全［M］. 上海：上海社会科学院出版社，2017.

［7］李宏娟，孙铮，姚茜. 邮轮面试英语［M］. 大连：大连海事大学出版社，2018.

［8］谢庆芳. 英语简历——求职入场券［M］. 北京：北京工业大学出版社，2016.

参 考 文 献